Every Child Deserves a Special Education

Every Child Deserves a Special Education

Five Mindframes That Ensure All Students Learn

Lee Ann Jung
Lorraine Graham
Nancy Frey
Douglas Fisher
John Hattie

CORWIN

FOR INFORMATION:

Corwin
A SAGE Company
2455 Teller Road
Thousand Oaks, California 91320
(800) 233-9936
www.corwin.com

SAGE Publications Ltd.
1 Oliver's Yard
55 City Road
London EC1Y 1SP
United Kingdom

SAGE Publications India Pvt. Ltd.
Unit No 323-333, Third Floor, F-Block
International Trade Tower Nehru Place
New Delhi 110 019
India

SAGE Publications Asia-Pacific Pte. Ltd.
18 Cross Street #10-10/11/12
China Square Central
Singapore 048423

Vice President and Editorial Director: Monica Eckman
Publisher: Jessica Allan
Senior Content Development Editor: Mia Rodriguez
Content Development and Operations Manager: Lucas Schleicher
Senior Editorial Assistant: Natalie Delpino
Project Editor: Amy Schroller
Copy Editor: Diana Breti
Typesetter: C&M Digitals (P) Ltd.
Cover Designer: Janet Kiesel
Marketing Manager: Olivia Bartlett

Printed and bound by CPI Group (UK) Ltd, Croydon, CR0 4YY

ISBN 9781071955260

This book is printed on acid-free paper.

25 26 27 28 29 10 9 8 7 6 5 4 3 2 1

Contents

About the Authors

Lee Ann Jung, PhD, is founder of Lead Inclusion, clinical professor at San Diego State University, and a consultant to schools worldwide. A former special education teacher and administrator, Lee Ann now spends her time in schools, working shoulder-to-shoulder with teams in their efforts to improve systems and practice. She has consulted with schools in more than thirty countries and throughout the United States in the areas of Universal Design for Learning, inclusion, intervention, and mastery assessment and grading. Lee Ann is the author of seven books, numerous journal articles, and book chapters on inclusion, universal design, and assessment. She serves as section editor of the *Routledge International Encyclopedia of Education* and on the editorial boards of several professional journals. In her community, Lee Ann is a board member for Life Adventure Center, a local nonprofit with a mission of healing for those who have experienced trauma.

Bring Lee Ann Jung to your school or district! Learn more at LeadInclusion.org.

Lorraine Graham, PhD, is foundation professor of Learning Intervention at The University of Melbourne. Lorraine began her career as a primary (elementary) teacher. She has written eight books and has a track record of scholarship in the areas of inclusive education and intervention research. Over the last thirty years, Lorraine has worked nationally and internationally with schools and school systems to support students with learning difficulties and deliver professional learning to teachers. In 2023, Lorraine was honored for significant service to education, particularly in the field of inclusive learning.

Nancy Frey is professor of educational leadership at San Diego State University and a leader at Health Sciences High and Middle College. Previously, Nancy was a teacher, academic coach, and central office resource coordinator in Florida. She is a credentialed special educator, reading specialist, and administrator in California. She is a member of the International Literacy Association's Literacy Research Panel. She has published widely on literacy, quality instruction, and assessment, as well as books such as *The Artificial Intelligence Playbook, How Scaffolding Works, Rigor Unveiled,* and *The Vocabulary Playbook.*

Douglas Fisher is professor and chair of educational leadership at San Diego State University and a leader at Health Sciences High and Middle College. Previously, Doug was an early intervention teacher and elementary school educator. He is a credentialed teacher and leader in California. In 2022, he was inducted into the Reading Hall of Fame by the Literacy Research Association. He has published widely on literacy, quality instruction, and assessment, as well as books such as *Welcome to Teaching, PLC+, Teaching Students to Drive Their Learning,* and *Student Assessment: Better Evidence, Better Decisions, Better Learning.*

John Hattie, PhD, is an award-winning education researcher and best-selling author with nearly thirty years of experience examining what works best in student learning and achievement. His research, better known as Visible Learning, is a culmination of nearly thirty years synthesizing more than 2,500 meta-analyses consisting of more than 150,000 studies involving more than 300 million students around the world. He has presented and keynoted at more than 300 international conferences and has received numerous recognitions for his contributions to education. His notable publications include *Visible Learning; Visible Learning for Teachers; Visible Learning and the Science of How We Learn; Visible Learning for Mathematics, Grades K–12;* and *10 Mindframes for Visible Learning.*

Introduction

We make a bold claim in the title of this book: *Every child deserves a special education*. Let's consider each of these words:

- Every child—not just some of the students and not just students who have been assessed and identified as having a disability
- Deserves—it's a right, inherent in public education, not reserved for some and not others
- Special—one that meets students' needs and challenges them to achieve greatness
- Education—meaning that students learn from the experiences we provide

And we believe this with all our hearts. Every one of our students, and your students, deserves an education that is special, one that has an impact, and one that they will remember. Thankfully, there is compelling evidence about what makes a special education. At the most basic level, a special education ensures that students are learning.

The question is, What truly makes a difference in student learning? Although the answers aren't always simple, we're fortunate to have an extraordinary evidence base that sheds light on this question. The *Visible Learning Meta*^{X} database, developed over 35 years, contains thousands of meta-analyses representing thousands of studies and millions of students (Corwin, 2024). It's updated a few times each year with new research, and to date, it identifies more than 450 influences on student learning. These influences are grouped into nine categories: student, home, school structure, classroom, curricula, teacher, teaching strategies, student learning strategies, and technology and out-of-school strategies.

However, the evidence doesn't stop at strategies and methods—it also tells a story about the power of educators' thinking about their work. Yes, we have teaching methods, but how we think about what we do significantly impacts the outcomes that follow. In the language of *Visible Learning*, these are called *mindframes*. Related concepts might include habits of mind, dispositions, or mindsets (Costa & Kallick, 2008; Zingoni & Corey, 2016). As the Peak Performance Center (2024) notes,

> Your mindset is your mental attitude or set of opinions that you have formed about something through experience, education, upbringing, and/or culture. You can have a mindset on a particular event, topic, item, or person.

Merriam-Webster defines a mindframe as "a mental attitude or outlook." The dictionary refers to mindframes as more than fleeting thoughts—they are deeply ingrained ways of thinking that influence behaviors and decisions. Mindframes and mindsets develop cyclically throughout our lives. We have thoughts based on our experiences. Those thoughts become our beliefs, which in turn impact our attitudes. Together, our thoughts, beliefs, and attitudes influence our actions and behaviors. These actions and behaviors create new experiences, which, in time, impact our thoughts, and the cycle starts again.

Consider this example of a challenge you might experience as a teacher with a particular student's learning: A colleague suggests that the student's struggles could stem from their diagnosis—let's say, intellectual disability. This provides an explanation for the challenge you're experiencing, which can shape your thinking. The risk is that you start to believe this is a common occurrence—that students who have intellectual disabilities are challenging to teach. This may, in turn, influence your attitude about inclusive classrooms, perhaps reinforcing the idea that some—or all—students with disabilities should be educated in separate settings designed to meet their particular needs. In a team meeting, this belief may lead you to recommend such a placement. In the classroom, it could result in lowered expectations for this student or reliance on a paraprofessional as the primary person to interact with the student.

Now, let's reimagine that scenario. This time, when you experience the challenge with that student's learning, a colleague describes how success might look for the student and suggests how various supports, such as technology, curriculum, and personnel, might be leveraged to improve outcomes. You review the student's prior performance and goals and identify times and places in your classroom that will allow the student to learn and practice activities that build the skills needed to reach these goals in the inclusive classroom. Your belief is, "This can work," and your attitude becomes, "Let's try!" You design instruction that incorporates the necessary supports, and soon you notice that these systems also benefit other students.

Your experience shifts: the student begins contributing positively to the classroom culture and makes meaningful progress toward Individual Education Program (IEP) goals. In IEP meetings, you share success stories and propose additional support for continued growth. In the classroom, you foster intentional peer engagement and carve out time for individual sessions with the student while the rest of the class works collaboratively and independently. You recognize that students facing the greatest learning challenges need regular access to expert instruction, and you make this a priority.

Developing your mindframe would take a completely different trajectory in these two scenarios. This book aims to use the *Visible Learning* research to identify the specific mindframes of educators who make a lasting difference. Explicitly cultivating these mindframes can help educators examine their experiences and actions, jumpstarting a cycle of reflection and growth that reshapes their thoughts, beliefs, and practices.

In this book, we focus on mindframes for those educators who support the learning of students with IEPs. That includes classroom teachers, paraprofessionals, advocates or special education teachers, related service providers, and leaders. But note from the title of this book that we believe that all learners deserve a special education, meaning engaging, effective, and impactful teaching and learning. As we will describe throughout this book, the systems of support we implement for specific students with specific documented needs are generally good for all students. When we intentionally implement support more universally, the positive impact extends far beyond any one individual student.

Before we dive into the mindframes that support effective inclusive classroom practices, it's important to understand how they connect to a larger framework. These mindframes align with and build on broader principles that guide teachers, families, leaders, and students in creating successful and supportive school environments. Figure i.1 illustrates how these mindframes work together (Hattie et al., 2024).

FIGURE I.1 Mindframes

MINDFRAMES

When it comes to impacting students' learning, it's less about what educators do and more about how we think about what we do. Educators' ways of thinking or mindsets, beliefs, and attitudes significantly influence the quality of education students receive. Visible Learning focuses on specific mindframes that influence how students, teachers, families, and leaders think. You can use these as a self-assessment tool, identify areas of strength, and plan on your own where to go next.

LEARNERS

I am confident that I can learn.

I set, implement, and monitor an appropriate mix of achieving and deep learning goals.

I strive to improve and enjoy my learning.

I strive to master and acquire surface and deep learning.

I work to contribute to a positive learning culture.

I know multiple learning strategies and know how best to use them.

I have the confidence and skills to learn from and contribute to group learning.

I can hear, understand, and action feedback.

I can evaluate my learning.

I am my own teacher.

TEACHERS

I am an evaluator of my impact on student learning.

I see assessment as informing my impact and next steps.

I collaborate with my peers and my students about my conceptions of progress and my impact.

I am a change agent and believe all students can improve.

I strive for challenge and not merely "doing my best."

I give and help students understand feedback, and I interpret and act on feedback given to me.

I engage as much in dialogue as in monologue.

I explicitly inform students what successful impact looks like from the outset.

I build relationships and trust so that learning can occur in a place where it is safe to make mistakes and learn from others.

I focus on learning and the language of learning.

LEADERS

I am an evaluator of my impact.

I see assessment as feedback to me.

I collaborate regarding my conceptions of progress and my progress.

I am a change agent.

I strive to challenge.

I give and help teachers understand feedback.

I engage as much in dialogue as monologue.

I explicitly inform teachers what successful impact looks like.

I build relationships and trust.

I focus on the language of learning.

FAMILY/CAREGIVER

I have appropriately high expectations.

I make reasonable demands and am highly responsive to my child.

I am not alone.

I develop my child's skill, will, and sense of thrill.

I love learning.

I know the power of feedback, and that success thrives on errors.

I am a parent, not a teacher.

I expose my child to language, language, language.

I appreciate that my child is not perfect, nor am I.

I am an evaluator of my impact.

BELONGING, IDENTITIES, AND EQUITY

We strive to invite all to learn.

We value engagement in learning.

We collaborate to learn and thrive.

We cultivate fortifying and sustaining environments for all identities.

We acknowledge, affirm, and embrace the identities of all our students.

We remove barriers to students' learning, including barriers related to identities.

We discover, correct, and disrupt inequities.

We embrace diverse cultures and identities.

We recognize and disrupt biases.

We create equitable opportunities and eliminate barriers to opportunities.

Each of the mindframes in Figure i.2 can and must be applied in inclusive classrooms. The first, and most critical, mindframe for all involved in education focuses on impact. The decisions that educators make should have a positive impact on students' learning. If not, educators need to change how they think and what they are doing to increase their impact. This is true regardless of whether a student has a diagnosis or an IEP. No matter their starting point or diagnosis, every student deserves to gain at least a year's growth given a year's input. Educators must understand what "at least" a year of learning looks like and then monitor their impact to ensure that they provide students with at least a year of learning. The notion of "at least" is key here, as many students (with and without IEPs) need more than a year's growth. It is almost a certainty, however, that if educators and students do not have high expectations for this rate of growth, it's unlikely to occur.

This connects directly to the second mindframe, which emphasizes the importance of assessment from multiple sources—such as tests, student work, assignments, and teacher and student judgments. Gathering, analyzing, and acting on this evidence is essential for improving student learning outcomes. Students risk stagnation without the teacher's belief in the value of assessment or a commitment to using it to guide instruction. They may be left repeating concepts they already understand, missing opportunities to build new skills, and losing any sense of progress or growth in their learning.

The mindframes apply to all educators but hold particular significance in inclusive classrooms. Dialogue—among educators and with students—is crucial, and collaboration with colleagues can amplify our impact on student learning. When educators develop a sense of collective responsibility, students benefit from the expertise and support of all teachers, not just those assigned to their classes. These mindframes remind us to move beyond outdated notions of "my students" and "your students." Instead, they reinforce the idea that all students are *our* students.

Relationships and trust are at the heart of another critical teacher mindframe. As others have noted, trust is the currency of the classroom (e.g., Bryk & Schneider, 2002). Strong teacher-student and student-student relationships create an environment where taking risks, making mistakes, and learning from errors is safe. Contrary to the misconception that students succeed simply because they like the teacher, the psychological safety created by strong relationships accelerates learning. This is why teachers need to develop strong growth-producing relationships with all of their students, especially those who aren't doing well in school. As Good (1987) showed decades ago, when teachers believe that students are low achieving, their actions toward those students are different. These actions harm relationships and hinder learning. For example, students labeled as low-achieving

- are criticized more often for failure,
- receive less feedback,
- are called on less often,
- have less eye contact with the teacher,
- have fewer friendly interactions with the teacher, and
- experience acceptance of their ideas less often.

FIGURE I.2 Mindframes for Teachers

1. I am an evaluator of my impact on student learning.
2. I see assessment as informing my impact and next steps.
3. I collaborate with my peers and my students about my conceptions of progress and my impact.
4. I am a change agent and believe all students can improve.
5. I strive for a challenge and not merely "doing my best."
6. I give and help students understand feedback, and I interpret and act on feedback given to me.
7. I engage as much in dialogue as monologue.
8. I explicitly inform students what successful impact looks like from the outset.
9. I build relationships and trust so that learning can occur in a place where it is safe to make mistakes and learn from others.
10. I focus on learning and the language of learning.

Source: Hattie and Zierer (2025).

Leaders, like teachers, also operate within critical mindframes (see Figure i.3). These mindframes apply to all students, both with and without IEPs. Just as teachers must evaluate their impact, leaders need to remain acutely aware of the effects of their decisions and take action when those effects fall short. Leaders play a pivotal role in shaping the climate and culture of every classroom and the school as a whole. They must engage in meaningful dialogue, build trusting relationships, and set the tone for inclusive and effective practices across their schools.

Two mindframes are particularly important for the leaders' work in inclusive schools. The first is that they are clear about how student success looks. At first glance, this may seem to center on ensuring that all students gain at least a year of growth for a year of school. Although this is, indeed, important, the concept of success extends beyond academic progress. Success can and should include the development of peer relationships, social skills, self-regulation, listening, and a host of other foundational learning skills. This is especially true for students with disabilities who may have missed opportunities to develop these essential skills earlier in life. Leaders carry the opportunity and responsibility of helping teachers and teams define success broadly and recognize the value in developing all of these skills alongside academic outcomes.

The second key mindframe for leaders involves shifting the conversation from one that focuses on teaching to one centered on the language of learning (Mindframe 10 for Leaders). Teaching strategies are important, but the focus must also include what and how students are learning and accomplishing each day, each week, each month, each semester, and each year. Just as teachers have success criteria for their classrooms, leaders should know what success looks like for the overall learning culture of their schools. By leading discussions about the learning taking place, leaders can build a shared understanding and collective responsibility for ensuring that every student has opportunities to succeed.

FIGURE I.3 Mindframes for Leaders

1. I am an evaluator of my impact.
2. I see assessment as feedback to me.
3. I collaborate regarding my conceptions of progress and my progress.
4. I am a change agent.
5. I strive to challenge myself and others.
6. I give and help teachers understand feedback.
7. I engage as much in dialogue as in monologue.
8. I explicitly inform teachers what successful impact looks like.
9. I build relationships and trust.
10. I focus on the language of learning.

Source: Hattie and Smith (2020).

In addition to mindframes for teachers and leaders, there are also mindframes designed for students and parents (Figure i.1). The key to parent mindframes is that parents see themselves not as first teachers (many do not have the specific skills of teachers) but as first learners—as parents learn, have expectations, deal with mistakes, and enjoy the struggles of learning, their children mimic this. Further, there are mindframes that focus on equity, identities, and belonging (see Figure i.4). These were identified through several rounds of research feedback from scholars worldwide using a process called Delphi. A team of educators drafted these mindframes and iteratively revised them based on extensive input from the research community (Law et al., 2024).

These mindframes explore the beliefs of educators regarding students who have often been marginalized, such as those from various racial/ethnic groups, religions, sexual orientations and gender identity groups, and disabilities. Like the mindframes presented earlier, the mindframes for equity, identities, and belonging apply to all students. But in this case, they represent thinking that needs to be ingrained into educators such that fairness becomes the norm in every classroom and school. Specifically, the students' concept of "this teacher is fair" is paramount.

Simply said, implicit biases that teachers may have about some groups of students impact their ability to learn. The students may be incorrect, and the teacher is fair, but their viewpoints or mindframes are critical—we need to know them before we can improve or modify them.

Factually speaking, there are inequities all around us. The challenge is to recognize them and then do something about them. For students with disabilities, referrals for services are inequitable (Katsiyannis et al., 2023), placement decisions are inequitable (Morgan et al., 2022), service delivery is inequitable (Friedman-Krauss & Barnett, 2023), discipline is inequitable (Zhang et al., 2004), and we could go on. Inclusive mindframes require that educators identify *and* disrupt these inequities.

The mindframes focus on embracing difference and disrupting bias. This is challenging work but necessary for our students' well-being. We all have biases, and we need to recognize and address them. And we need to embrace the wonderful diversity that exists in our world. It sounds like a slogan, but it's true: Diversity is our strength. We need diversity of people's experiences, ideas, and beliefs to make us all stronger.

Relatedly, educators with equity mindframes recognize that there are barriers for many students that must be addressed. We need to increase the opportunities to learn and eliminate as many barriers as possible for all students. This applies equally to students with disabilities who face a number of barriers to their learning and participation. Equity mindframes demand that we recognize these inequities and work to eliminate barriers.

There are also mindframes related to the identities of our students. In the past, differences were something to hide, to feel ashamed of, and to be embarrassed about. That has to change and is changing. Differences, including those that fit the definition of disability, are part of the human experience, and all people are well served when they embrace their identities, including how they experience the world. Disability identity can be described as a "sense of self that includes one's disability and feelings of connection to, or solidarity with, the disability community" (Dunn & Burcaw, 2013, p. 148). In an investigation of the aspects of disability identity, Forber-Pratt et al. (2020) noted the following four factors: internal beliefs about one's own disability and the disability community; anger and frustration with disability experiences; adoption of disability community values; and contribution to the disability community. Educators who embrace this mindframe help students integrate their differences into their identities.

Another powerful mindframe focuses on belonging and requires that educators invite all students to learn. We interpret this to mean educating students with identified needs in inclusive classrooms, with support, such that they can learn alongside their peers. Unfortunately, a prevalent counter-mindframe maintains that students with more significant needs are "better off" with others with the same label or need. The idea seems to be that educators can customize the learning experiences based on the needs of their students. But the reality is that it doesn't work this way. The evidence is clear: students learn better when they are educated in inclusive settings. As we will explore later, inclusive education positively impacts learning outcomes, with an effect size of 0.32. And this is based on 445 studies that involved more than 4.8 million students.

FIGURE I.4 Mindframes for Equity, Identities, and Belonging

1. We discover, correct, and disrupt inequities.
2. We embrace diverse cultures and identities.
3. We recognize and disrupt biases.
4. We create equitable opportunities and eliminate barriers to opportunities.
5. We cultivate fortifying and sustaining environments for all identities.
6. We acknowledge, affirm, and embrace the identities of all our students.
7. We remove barriers to students' learning, including barriers related to identities.
8. We strive to invite all to learn.
9. We value engagement in learning.
10. We collaborate to learn and thrive.

Source: Law et al. (2024).

In the following chapters, we organize the narrative into five mindframes for inclusive classrooms that compel us to plan for not only a diverse pool of learners in our schools but also the diversity within each learner. As we present these mindframes for inclusive education, it is important to clarify who we're talking about. The answer is both specific and expansive. Studies conducted with students who have disabilities or IEPs are central to these conversations, as these students face some of the most significant barriers to learning. However, these are not the only students who experience barriers and benefit from the mindframes we outline. Many learners have substantial needs that fall just short of qualifying for formal support; some face greater barriers in some subjects than in other subjects, or with some teachers and not others; and some face long-term barriers, while others have short-term needs (e.g., as a consequence of death in the family or an extended illness). Students face barriers related to language acquisition, trauma, moving, family dynamics, and the list goes on.

Although many of these students do not have a diagnosis or an IEP, their needs are just as pressing—and the mindframes explored in this book are equally effective for them. In fact, what we've learned from designing practices that work for students with disabilities provides valuable lessons for serving all learners. Inclusive practices—those that prioritize access, equity, and engagement—are not limited to one group. Instead, they have a ripple effect, improving the educational experience for everyone in the classroom.

Far from abstract, the five mindframes we present are pragmatic, actionable approaches anchored in a robust foundation of research. For each mindframe, we provide specific learning intentions and success criteria and a range of teaching scenarios for illustration and reflective practice. We'll invite you to assess your understanding of each mindframe. As we progress through each chapter, remember that these mindframes are more than lenses for viewing a change in methods—a change in *doing*. They are catalysts for changes in *thinking* that will lead to better learning experiences and outcomes for students.

Every Child Is Special

1

Learning Intentions

- I am learning about student variability and the value of inclusive environments.
- I am learning about Universal Design for Learning (UDL) as a framework to anticipate and address barriers to student learning.

Success Criteria

- I can describe variation in terms of a jagged profile that we all have.
- I can describe how instructional design grounded in UDL principles benefits all students.
- I can plan my instruction from the assumption that there will always be variance in my class.

Each of us is a magnificent "proprietary blend" of interests, abilities, values, needs, and experiences that make us who we are as beautifully unique individuals. We can see some of the variation between people, like in their height or facial features. But the most complex and interesting diversity lives within our minds. This pattern of variation we each have is as dynamic as it is unique. The areas in which you excel today might require nurturing tomorrow, and the challenges you face now could turn into your greatest strengths down the line.

In his 2016 book, *The End of Average*, Todd Rose explores the complexity of human variation. He introduces the concept of a "jagged profile" to illustrate the variation *between* and *within* individuals. The two students in Figure 1.1 have some similarities in their profiles; maybe they even have the same grades. But these two students also have jagged profiles—just as we all do—that make them unique. This notion of a jagged profile avoids the use of words loaded with positive or negative attributes; other terms could be mosaic minds, talent tapestry, capability canvas, the skill-scape, or talent terrain—although we prefer the term *jagged profile*.

FIGURE 1.1 Jagged Profiles

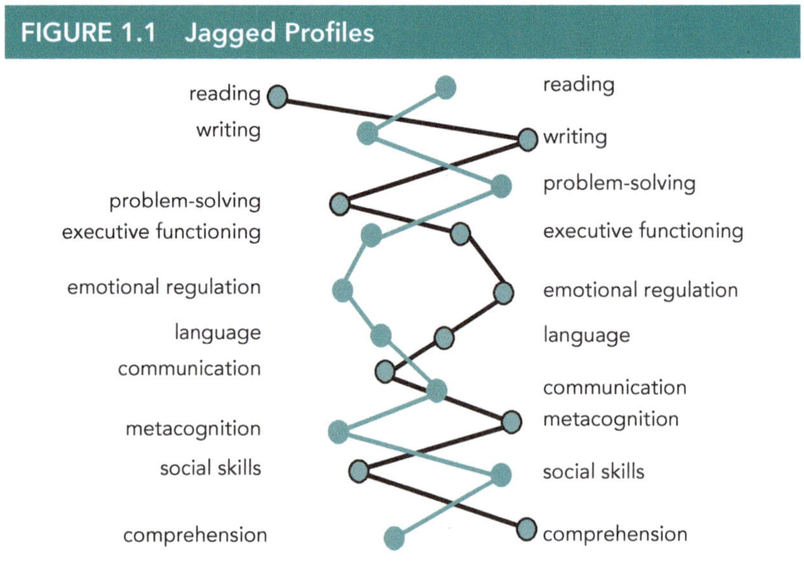

When thinking about students' jagged profiles, elements like literacy, problem-solving, behavior, and critical thinking may come to mind because those are the ones that lead to grades or formal feedback. However, other parts of our profile are equally important, such as metacognition, emotional regulation, executive function, and compassion. For many of our students, one or more points on their jagged profiles diverge significantly from the typical range. They could be soaring past expectations or facing hurdles that require extra support. Needs for support or challenge can appear in academic, social, or emotional domains and signal us to take notice and make a plan. Consider the variety in these student profiles:

- **Liam, seventh grade:** Liam is a prodigy in coding, often losing himself in the world of algorithms and programming languages. His room is decorated with tech posters, and he dreams of creating the next big video game. Liam struggles with emotional regulation and becomes easily frustrated when things don't go as planned. He has a wicked sense of humor and loves sharing tech jokes with his friends.
- **Logan, sixth grade:** Logan has an intellectual disability and learns best through videos and hands-on models. He is curious and loves exploring how things work, often taking apart gadgets at home to see what's inside. Logan enjoys outdoor activities and has a gentle, kind-hearted nature. His enthusiasm for life is infectious, and he thrives when he can use his senses to understand the concepts being taught.
- **Ava, third grade:** Ava has needs in spatial reasoning and benefits greatly from support with geometric concepts. She has a vivid imagination and loves creating intricate drawings and building elaborate structures with her Lego sets. Ava is a quiet, observant child who enjoys solving puzzles and playing strategy games. She excels when learning is connected to visual and tactile experiences.
- **Emma, fifth grade:** Emma has debilitating social anxiety, making it challenging for her to interact with peers and participate in class. She is currently working with a counselor to gain new interaction strategies. Emma is an avid reader and finds solace in the pages of fantasy novels. She has a gentle demeanor and is incredibly empathetic, often volunteering to help animals at the local shelter.
- **Muhammad, second grade:** Muhammad needs support with reading but shows extraordinary musical aptitude. He is ready to compose and explore complex music theory and is often seen with his keyboard or guitar. Muhammad has an infectious enthusiasm for music and loves performing for his family. His vibrant personality shines through his music, and he eagerly shares his melodies with others.

- **Mia, first grade:** Mia has significant short-term memory needs and requires support to learn strategies for following routines and instructions for everyday tasks. She has a rich imagination and loves storytelling and role-playing games. Mia enjoys all types of visual art, often creating elaborate projects to decorate her room. Her energetic personality and love for all things creative help her engage with learning.
- **José, tenth grade:** José has executive functioning needs but demonstrates unparalleled storytelling abilities. He needs opportunities to craft narratives with professional-level depth and complexity. José is a charismatic teenager with a passion for writing, often staying up late to pen his thoughts and stories. He is also a member of the drama club, where his storytelling skills shine on stage. José's ability to generate intricate tales captivates his audience, and he benefits from structured support to manage his time and organize his ideas effectively.

Each of these students qualifies for special education services, but as we can see, this is where their commonalities end. There aren't any substantive needs that are the same for this group of students. When we see students as "special education students," rather than seeing each student's jagged profile, we run the very real risk of leading to sweeping and formulaic decisions based on labels instead of making intentional decisions that respond to each student's strengths, interests, and needs. The ramifications are far-reaching, affecting both how students see themselves and the opportunities they have in school. The most ubiquitous example of this type of sweeping decision based on the label of "special education student" is found within the confines of the resource room, where students with IEPs are grouped together, regardless of their specific needs.

From the Classroom

An Inefficient Grouping

Ms. Jackson walks into her special education resource room with a mixture of determination and frustration. It was the same routine at 1:15 every day when she gathered her crew of nine eighth graders, each with their own unique needs. The only common thread among them is that they have IEPs.

As students trickle in, Ms. Jackson greets each one with a kind smile. The bell rings, and the room buzzes with activity. Ms. Jackson begins circulating the room, addressing questions and helping with assignments. She's a skilled interventionist, but she's expected to help each student keep up with assignments, often sacrificing deeper support for their specific needs.

She glances at Alex, focused intensely on his reading passage with concern apparent in his brows. "Ms. Jackson, I'm having trouble with this part." She knows Alex needs more than just homework help; he needs a structured reading intervention for which she simply doesn't have the time.

Priya raises her hand, confused by the math problem in front of her. "I don't understand this math problem at all." Ms. Jackson moves toward Priya. "Let's untangle it together, Priya." She offers explanations, but she knows that Priya's struggles with number sense run deeper, and she wishes she could provide the targeted support Priya deserves.

Then there's Liam, who's having a particularly rough day. "This is stupid!" he yelled, his emotions spilling over. Ms. Jackson wishes she could dedicate time to teaching Liam the emotional regulation strategies he needs to cope with overwhelm, but how can she take time to teach him strategies when the others in the room have different needs?

As the day progresses, Ms. Jackson's feelings of frustration and defeat grow. In her heart, she knows that her students can do much more than just complete assignments. They deserve a chance to receive tailored interventions to develop essential skills.

In Ms. Jackson's class, students were grouped together because they were "special education students." But Alex, Priya, and Liam all need different types of support or intervention. It makes logical sense to group students who share the same needs for intervention flexibly. Grouping students with varying needs in a special education classroom for support time creates an impossible situation for teachers. It prevents students from accessing the skills-based intervention they truly need.

It's a massive mistake to ignore the individual points within students' jagged profiles and see them as fitting neatly into the broad categories of having an IEP or being gifted. The language of this error rings loudly through the halls of our schools when we hear "special education kid" alongside its many variations: "IEP kid," "Inclusion student," or "Ashley's kids." **Let's set the record straight: There's no such thing as a "special education kid."** Sure, there are students who receive special education services, but special education isn't something a student *is*. There isn't a *type* of student who is a special education student. All students are general education students. And all deserve to receive an education that responds to their jagged profiles. All students are special.

Recognizing the jagged profile of each student requires us to be agile educators for all students. We look at both the quantitative assessments and the qualitative insights—those nuanced moments in the classroom, the candid chats at parent-teacher conferences, and the students' own reflections on their learning experiences. Armed with these rich understandings, we make decisions about what each student needs. So, what about that student battling emotional storms? Time for focused emotional support. And the young writer who's penning stories like the next Margaret Atwood? We've got to step it up and give these students challenges worthy of their talents. Each student's needs should inform the selection of high-leverage strategies; for the most part, these strategies can be applied to all students or as options for all students. When we take this dynamic approach to understanding our students, we honor our students' unique profiles, respect their individuality, and set the stage for them to achieve phenomenal growth. This does not mean that we have to individualize all learning experiences for each student continually. Rather, we can design universal approaches that meet many needs, bringing efficiency to our efforts and broadening the scope of our support.

Necessary for Some, Good for All

Ramps, curb cuts, lever door handles, elevators, wider doors, braille, and audible signals at crosswalks are all around us. But unless you require these accessibility features, they are probably not something you think about all that often. Other than braille, every item on that list is a feature that benefits everyone. You've absolutely benefitted from an elevator, whether or not you use a wheelchair. The same goes for ramps, wider doorways, larger bathrooms, and crosswalk signals. You've used and benefited from every one of those accessibility features, and, at times, you may have *needed* them.

This principle of universal design—creating solutions that are necessary for some but beneficial for all—extends beyond physical spaces and into educational practices. When we take the time to dive into special education research, we find a vault of information for enhancing teaching quality for all students. Just as accessibility features in buildings benefit all of us, the mindframes in this book make an enormous difference for students with disabilities but also benefit every student. Rather than seeing the wisdom from special education research as a specialized toolkit for a specific group, we aim to use the lessons learned from special education research as a roadmap for elevating instructional quality across the board. Our aim is to highlight actionable insights that can transform each classroom into a more effective learning environment.

Indeed, the evidence shows that the practices that work for those receiving special education services are beneficial for all, but going about this the other way doesn't have the same effect. When we design our instruction, especially initial instruction, for those who engage and learn easily, we leave all the students who don't learn as easily behind. Some students will even learn when given poor instruction. Thus, the most authentic evidence of the quality of instruction is found in the students who *don't* have the easiest time learning—not in the students who are going to learn no matter what.

Special education research is where we have uncovered the highest leverage practices that work for the most intractable educational challenges. The majority of these effective strategies that work for those with the greatest needs can bring powerful results when brought into the classroom and used with all students. The way reading instruction has evolved over the years is a perfect example. Some students learn to read with little evidence-based reading instruction at all—they seem to develop the ability from just being exposed to print and interactions with well-meaning adults. But we can't look to those students for evidence about teaching all students to read. When we study reading instruction practices with students who have the most difficulty learning to read, we discover what works. When we bring those practices that work with those students who have the biggest needs into every classroom to use with every student, now we're getting somewhere!

Special education strategies shouldn't be relegated to a corner reserved for a select few. Instead, these universal strategies benefit every student, irrespective of their needs. This book is about realizing that these methods and insights aren't just "necessary for some" but can be game-changers for all. With these excellent teaching practices, we can meet most of the needs on everyone's jagged profile. Strategies like small group instruction or using mnemonics are necessary for some and great for everyone. This doesn't take away the fact that some students have unique needs. The orientation and mobility needs of a blind student are an example. Educators still have to address those needs. But when we do a great job with UDL, we can focus our individualization efforts at those times when they are *really* needed rather than trying to individualize everything.

Imagine a classroom where instruction is crafted with the highest leverage practices that address the biggest needs in mind, where teachers plan inclusively from the beginning and work together. That's the power of tapping into the wisdom of special education. Special education research is a pathway guiding us toward a limitless future for *all* learners. Next, let's discover the influences that can supercharge our inclusive toolkit.

Thinking Strategically

High-leverage practices are the foundation of the most impactful teaching, offering powerful tools to address diverse student needs and boost learning outcomes. However, truly effective teaching involves more than adding additional strategies; it requires that we

1. understand our students' jagged profiles, including their strengths and assets,
2. anticipate the diverse challenges they might experience,
3. select the optimal strategies related to (1) and (2),

4. proactively implement these high-leverage practices that address the possible barriers to learning, and
5. continually evaluate the impact of our choice of strategies on the learning lives of our students.

Strategic thinking means planning, true to UDL, with the assumption that student variability is the norm, not the exception (CAST, 2024).

Imagine a teacher planning for the upcoming math instructional unit by paying attention to the variation in their students. They recognize that some students might feel they can't do it, others might find it boring, and some might already be ahead of the curve. Thinking strategically, this teacher provides students with multiple ways to engage with the material. Rather than primarily using whole-group instruction, the classroom becomes a hub of collaborative group activity, with students using visuals and models to grasp complex concepts, engaging in hands-on activities, and exploring applications of math. Digital tools are available for students to learn at varied paces, catering to those who need more time and those ready for advanced challenges. By anticipating these varied needs, the teacher ensures that all students are engaged, supported, learning, and challenged. Notice that the teacher didn't create different difficulty levels but enabled multiple ways to access and matriculate through the material to support every student's learning journey.

High-leverage practices rooted in special education research are key in this strategic approach. These practices, proven effective for students with significant learning needs, can elevate the quality of instruction for all students when thoughtfully integrated into the classroom. The goal is to embed these practices into the core of our teaching methods, ensuring our instruction is inclusive, effective, efficient, and adaptable. The result is an inclusive learning environment so robust that fewer students need specially designed instruction or adaptations. By recognizing the diversity within our classrooms and planning proactively, we can leverage the best practices from special education and all education research to benefit all students. As we delve into mindframes for inclusive education throughout this book, remember that thinking strategically is critical, adaptive expertise should become the norm, and we are devoted to thinking evaluatively about what we do.

Summary

Labels and disability categories aren't what makes a child special. *Every* child is indeed special because of their unique profiles of abilities, interests, personalities, and needs. The profiles for some students are so multidimensional that they have significant needs for support in one area and just as significant needs for challenge in another—and on some days but not on others, in some subjects and not in others, in some contexts but not in others. These profiles are fluid! The notion that students with learning needs are outliers is outdated. The truth is, the farthest points on the jagged profiles can be crowded places! Diversity isn't a challenge to be managed; it's our greatest asset in a rich educational environment—and society. Our responsibility and privilege as educators is to recognize this individuality and respond with proactive, inclusive, and evidence-based instruction that has a marked positive impact on learning and achievement.

High-leverage practices rooted in special education research are invaluable to this strategic approach. These practices, proven effective for students with significant learning needs, elevate the quality of instruction for all students when thoughtfully integrated into classrooms. By embedding these practices into our teaching methods, we create robust, inclusive learning environments where fewer students need specially designed instruction or adaptations.

As we continue through this book, remember that effective teaching involves more than simply implementing these strategies. It requires anticipating challenges, understanding student variability, and thinking strategically to create an inclusive and supportive learning environment. In embracing the mindframe that every child is special, we commit to seeing past labels and view variation as a normal part of the human condition. In doing so, our task is clear: We must design every unit and every lesson with an eye on the jagged profile.

Learning Check

I can describe the variation in terms of a jagged profile that we all have.

STRONGLY DISAGREE	DISAGREE	NEUTRAL	AGREE	STRONGLY AGREE
1	2	3	4	5

I can describe how instructional design grounded in UDL principles benefits all students.

STRONGLY DISAGREE	DISAGREE	NEUTRAL	AGREE	STRONGLY AGREE
1	2	3	4	5

I can plan my instruction assuming there will always be variance in my class.

STRONGLY DISAGREE	DISAGREE	NEUTRAL	AGREE	STRONGLY AGREE
1	2	3	4	5

All Students Can Achieve at High Levels

2

Learning Intentions

- I'm learning about the impact of teacher expectations on students' learning.
- I'm learning about the value of inclusive environments for the growth and achievement of all students.

Success Criteria

- I can describe the potential harm caused by labeling students and how it can lead to lowered expectations and segregated placements.
- I can explain with evidence why inclusive classrooms benefit all students, including those with and without disabilities.
- I can identify and evaluate moments when I may have allowed labels or assumptions to influence expectations and adjust my approach to be more inclusive and empowering.

In 2021, Lee Ann delivered professional development in a small, rural school in Utah where a powerful story unfolded—one that would forever shift the faculty's perspective on inclusion and the power of teacher expectations. A new fourth-grade student joined the school, arriving without any academic records. His teachers didn't take long to realize he was significantly behind in literacy, communication, and math skills, essentially on a first-grade level across the curriculum. The teachers worked to develop a solid plan of how to support this student with a thoughtful mix of differentiation, modifications, and intensive intervention. His teachers also added the most important ingredient—they believed in him.

In an impressively short time, the boy's progress met and then exceeded the team's expectations. He thrived in his fourth-grade classroom and went from requiring intensive intervention to minimal support, all within a single academic year. Incredible, right? Well, just when everyone thought the story couldn't become more inspirational, his past academic records arrived. Everyone was stunned at what they saw. The student had spent four years—his entire educational journey—in a segregated special education classroom. He'd never spent time in an inclusive classroom.

Here was undeniable evidence, right there in their own building, that their team's expectations had the power to transform. Because they didn't know about his previous placement, their expectations weren't influenced to believe he couldn't succeed in an inclusive classroom. The student rose to their expectations. We aren't sure how we'd find the postal workers who caused the delay in this student's package of paperwork, but we'd sure like to thank them. The lag in that delivery changed the trajectory of this young person's life. We wonder how many students sitting in segregated classrooms today would meet the same success in inclusive settings if their teachers didn't know the history of their placements.

Labels as Opportunity Thieves

We can make informed guesses about how labels, expectations, and segregated settings interact. Labels lead to segregated settings. Segregated settings lead to lowered expectations. Students perform poorly when the expectations are lower. The results of lowered expectations validate segregated settings—a disaster in the making (Figure 2.1).

FIGURE 2.1 A Disastrous Intersection

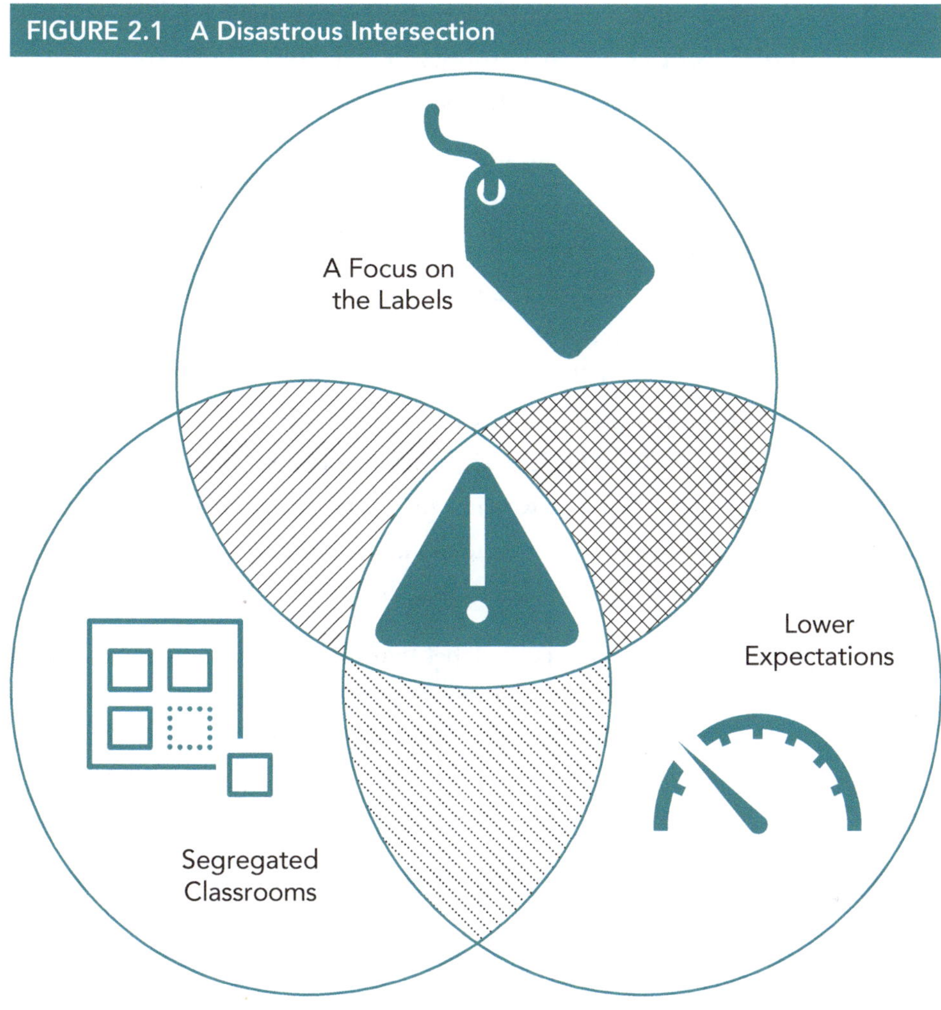

When we use labels, we can start to believe that these labels—these shorthand codes for complex human experiences—somehow predict potential. But labels can't capture the essence of a person, nor do they reflect the unique strengths each student brings to the table. Although labels might give us a path to determine eligibility for certain services, they're far from the whole story. Labels can be a quick way to communicate a likely pattern of needs, but to make assumptions about any individual student from the label is a mistake. Characteristics associated with autism spectrum conditions (ASC), for example, include an array of assets and needs, but no two people with ASC are alike. Having a label doesn't take away the fact that each person has a unique jagged profile. For this reason, our focus should be on specific strengths and needs, not the label, when discussing supports, services, and placement.

Doug attended a side-by-side school with a campus for students with significant disabilities located across a small moat from the comprehensive high school. The students from the segregated school crossed the bridge each day to clean the cafeteria following lunch. Thus, the students in the comprehensive school saw the students with significant disabilities on a daily basis but were not given the chance to interact with them. The only students who were allowed to interact were those who took an elective class, which Doug did because he was given the choice of peer tutoring, Russian, or animal husbandry. The perspective was that only specialized professionals and trained peers could interact with students with significant disabilities.

Intellectual disability is the label that most often leads to segregated placements like this. But just because students have an intellectual disability and gaps academically doesn't mean they need to be in segregated, special education settings. Without a foundation of inclusion, some of the most meaningful outcomes of the school experience, and life, are lost.

Compare Doug's high school experience with Lee Ann's. Lee Ann grew up in the Deep South, and in her small town, church was where most people found a sense of community. As a part of her church community, Lee Ann spent time with thirty or so young people from the time they were in elementary school through high school graduation. Over the years, and as they grew into adolescence, the cohesion of the group only tightened. They truly were like family.

One of the members of this youth group was Todd. Todd was an incredibly important part of the group. He brought such positivity, energy, and silliness. And Todd had a significant intellectual disability. Of course, the group was aware of his cognitive difference, but there was never a question of whether Todd would be included. He was there every week for the regularly scheduled events, but also the beach trips, ski trips, and the big choir tour to Chicago. Todd was always there, included as an important member of the group.

Todd had a crush on Lee Ann for a while. Her maiden name was "Moore," and Todd frequently joked in front of the group, "Lee, Lee, Lee Ann Moore, I love you, too, you love me more." He'd cover a wide smile with his hand, look at her with a silly "side eye," and the whole group laughed. Every. Single. Time.

Here's the part of this that comes back to Lee Ann over and over now as an educator. There was no IEP at church. There was no special educator. They all felt they belonged. They all just did it, the adults and the kids. And they did a fantastic job of meaningful inclusion. Could they have had a stronger impact had they been armed with evidence-based practices? Probably. But Todd was in a segregated classroom at school, and no one in his youth group ever saw him there. I think we'd all be comfortable taking a bet on where Todd gained the most valuable learning.

Imagine now, you go to your doctor not feeling well. She makes you complete a blood test, undergo some scans, and fill out a medical diary. Then, upon returning, the doctor pronounces you have disease X—and says now my job is done! You would be horrified. The point is that labeling can serve as a starting point, but the essence is in the following interventions—did they ameliorate the symptoms, did they lead to better health, and did the intervention have a used-by date when you were feeling well again? In education, so often, labels become fixed, define the person, set boundaries, and improve little. Labels set expectations not only for educators but also for students. Too often, these are low expectations, which are devastating; they lead to restricted opportunities and invite setting "easy" tasks to buttress self-beliefs, which in turn defend, promote, and reinforce low expectations. Labels become an excuse for why the student "cannot" and not just first steps to interventions. Labeling that leads to successful intervention has a place, but it needs to be tied to the success of the intervention, should most often be temporary, and should be based on high expectations.

Upon diagnosing an ailment, the doctor does not define the person as a cancer person, a heart problem, and so on. Diagnosis is specific to need. Yes, we can learn from interventions with many previous cancer and heart patients and their successes, but what matters is the application of this knowledge specifically to this patient, here and now.

The point of this story isn't to suggest that we shouldn't have plans with individualized strategies. A body of research developed over many years has taught us strategies that work for students with intellectual disabilities, those who have learning disabilities, those on the autism spectrum, and those with many other labels with similar patterns of needs. These strategies are "high probability" interventions, and the success is the degree to which they improve students' learning—not that they must be applied because the label matches specific interventions.

This journey from labels as opportunity thieves to optimal practices as liberators showcases the necessity and the beauty of seeing every student as an individual with a jagged profile and as a valuable member of the community. The power of this transition in thinking is lived and breathed in stories like Todd's and in countless classrooms around the world. In these narratives, we see the limitless futures for students when we release our confidence in labels and lean on natural supports, peer relationships, and high-leverage instructional practices.

Students with identified disabilities and those who are behind grade level are not the only students who have needs. A label of "high ability" or "gifted" can also change the course of expectations—and how we support students. Those with a label of high ability may not show outward signs of struggle, but they can be fighting a different battle—a battle against boredom, isolation, and the slow erosion of their innate love for learning. They can battle against the fear of failure, the pressures from others who expect that they always excel, and the worry of imposter syndrome, where they may be big fish in little ponds today but could become little fish in big ponds in another context. Some students may feel different and misunderstood by classmates. They may mask their ease of learning to blend in or to avoid bullying.

Some students come to us with such an extraordinarily high level of skill and understanding that without excellent universal design and differentiation, they become inadequately challenged in their classrooms. High-performing students often learn faster and want to dig deeper into topics. These students are at risk for lack of engagement in longer blocks of large-group instruction that lags in pace relative to their understanding. An appropriately challenging curriculum isn't a "nice to have"; ensuring that every student is given the Goldilocks level of challenge (not too hard, not too easy, and not too boring) is predictive of learning outcomes (d = 0.60; Corwin, 2024). A consistent lack of challenge can ultimately sap high-ability students' natural love of learning, curiosity, and self-direction as learners. As a result, their interests and talents can be left underdeveloped. But this skill to understand and arrange the Goldilocks level of challenge applies to ALL students.

Boredom resulting from lack of appropriate challenge doesn't only feel unpleasant; it has a demonstrated negative impact on learning (d = –0.46; Corwin, 2024). Spiraling content, an important universal design strategy for comprehension and memory retrieval, can feel like unnecessary repetition. Some high-ability students cope with the resulting boredom by skating by with minimal effort, doing just enough to get "good" or "good enough" grades but not truly engaging in learning.

Boredom is the most cited negative emotion in classes across all students (Blannin et al., 2024). This is most often a consequence of the work being too easy, and we note Graham Nuthall's (2007) finding that in most classes, 40–50 percent of students can already do the work that is being assigned. Boring. Here's the good news: There are solutions we can put into place in every class to kick the boredom. This first requires us to be aware of which students experience boredom and understand their optimal level of challenge. Was the work so hard that they did not bother? Or was it too easy and there was no joy in learning?

Thinking about the students who get straight A's, it's natural to think they've figured it all out. But these students aren't necessarily free from experiencing risk or challenge. High-performing students are often the most susceptible to mental health crises. The American Psychological Association (2015) isn't mincing words here—they've reported that high-achieving students are particularly susceptible to intense academic pressure, which can result in feelings of despair, burnout, and, in extreme cases, suicidal thoughts.

Because of the pressure to maintain status or avoid failure, some students begin to settle into patterns of perfectionism. As a society, we joke about, trivialize, and even celebrate perfectionism. We tune in to watch in amazement as Marie Kondo alphabetizes spice racks and color-coordinates sock drawers, and we all wish we could be so organized. But the pursuit of "perfect" is a well-documented pathway to mental health crises (Flett & Hewitt, 2014). The five of us have seen the result of celebrating perfectionism in our schools as students clamor for the highest grades and GPAs in high school. This orientation shifts the focus away from learning to playing the game of school perfectly. High-stakes testing, final exams, and "big" projects can pile on distressing pressure. Any additional demands from parents can quickly breed crushing anxiety. On the surface, perfectionism may appear to be an asset or admirable trait, but make no mistake: Perfectionism in school is maladaptive and is likely to have a negative impact on learning (d = -0.03; Corwin, 2024). Even the "high ability" label can shift our attention away from unmet needs.

Perhaps it is no surprise that the majority of "gifted" students do not become "gifted" adults. Indeed, fewer than 2 percent of child prodigies become adult prodigies (Winner, 2000; Subotnik, 2009). Howard (2008, pp. 119–120), for example, noted that there is "little apparent link between being a prodigy and becoming eminent . . . and some recognized geniuses, such as Albert Einstein, reportedly showed no early signs of great talent." Herb Marsh and colleagues (1995) have extensively documented the negative effects of being labeled gifted. He found that students in gifted and talented programs experienced significant declines in academic self-concept over time when compared to students not in these gifted classes.

A key issue is to be aware of students' beliefs about themselves and ensure that there is never the claim that a singular type of intervention has a common effect on students with a particular label. It is more likely that most students need a higher level of challenge in one area, and require intervention in another area. Imagine a student devouring books like a literary critic but stuck with multiplication. Or another who's a problem-solving wizard but melts down at the hint of conflict. What about the learner who is gifted in metacognition, keenly aware of their own learning strategies, yet their social skills are developing more slowly?

From the Classroom

Rosa's Unmet Needs

Rosa sat in the back of Mrs. Bernal's third-grade classroom, doodling intricate fractal patterns on the corners of her notebook. The room hummed with the sound of children practicing their skills with fractions using number lines, yet Rosa's mind was miles away, engrossed in an advanced fantasy novel she'd discovered in the library.

Mrs. Bernal, circulated the room, checking on progress and offering feedback and encouragement. Rosa's paper was blank, except for her doodles in the margins. "Rosa, you need to get started," she said, her voice tinged with concern but also a bit of frustration. To Mrs. Bernal, Rosa seemed self-sufficient, just lost in her world of numbers, dragons, and lore.

Rosa was quick to scribble answers in her notebook, but she felt she didn't fit in anywhere in school, sandwiched between her unmet potential and unaddressed needs. Her mind was a firework display of thoughts and ideas, bursting with complex questions about the universe, social justice, and the patterns she saw in everything. Yet, basic arithmetic felt like trying to catch smoke with her hands.

Because Rosa used words like "enigmatic" and "paradox," Mrs. Bernal mistook this for universal competence. She misinterpreted the mistakes in Rosa's math work as "careless errors." She never suspected that Rosa, who had this astonishing vocabulary and read books way above her grade level, might also have a significant need.

In a world that loves labels, Rosa is both gifted and has a learning disability. Instead of implementing strategies to address Rosa's profile of both gifts and challenges, Rosa's significant educational needs were left unaddressed. The assumptions around need can go the other way, too. Sometimes, students who have identified disabilities miss out on opportunities for enrichment or acceleration because the disability is all that's seen.

Lee Ann remembers when her older child, who had been labeled as having a learning disability, was in middle school. He was intrigued and interested in world cultures, economies, and languages and wanted to take Mandarin. He'd made amazing progress in reading and writing, but the team knew learning another language would be challenging for him. The conversation that normally follows this dilemma often takes all of about two minutes. The team's experience suggests that the student wouldn't be able to pass or perform like the other students, and, therefore, the additional language class isn't appropriate. The disability is all that's noticed.

Fortunately, that's not how the eighth-grade team approached the question for Lee Ann's child. They never questioned whether he could take the course. They agreed without discussion that he would take it. They weren't focused on the grade-level standards and a disability label. They saw her child and the high abilities in his jagged profile, and importantly, they saw his interests. They saw him. Not the label. Could he gain valuable learning in Mandarin class, even though mastering eighth-grade standards for the course may not happen? Absolutely. And he did.

Taking a world language is often the first course omitted from the curriculum for a student with a label. But these language classes can have a significant positive impact on students' outcomes (d = 0.85; Corwin, 2024). Assuming that because a student has a label that these positive benefits aren't available should make us all take a step backward and revise our low expectations.

Do you know a little bit of a language that you aren't fluent in? Do you know about other world cultures but don't speak the associated languages? Can you speak words and phrases in another language but can't write them well? By simply changing the question around placement, we can open new doors for students with learning differences rather than closing them unnecessarily because of a label.

This is the least dangerous assumption: that the student will benefit from the experiences planned in a given class. The most dangerous assumption is that the student will not benefit and should not be afforded the opportunity to do so. In 1984, Anne Donnellan, a respected researcher in special education, wrote that "the criterion of least dangerous assumption holds that in the absence of conclusive data, educational decisions ought to be based on assumptions which, if incorrect, will have the least dangerous effect on the likelihood that students will be able to func-tional independently as adults" (p. 141). Furthermore, she concluded, "we should assume that poor performance is due to instructional inad-equacy rather than to student deficits" (p. 147). The team supporting Lee Ann's child made a decision using the least dangerous assumption and it turned out that her child benefited significantly. But what if that had not been the case and the benefits were not as powerful? Her child still had the benefits of communication and interaction opportunities and cultural experiences. After all, how many of us remember all of the content we were taught in middle school or high school? Thankfully, no one made decisions about our rights to be in regular class or thwarted our opportunities to be educated alongside our peers.

Expecting Successful Inclusion

The continuum of placement options ranges from schools that only enroll students with disabilities, like the one next to Doug's high school, to classrooms that serve only students with disabilities, like the class-room where Todd was, to inclusive "general education" classrooms that support students in general education classes. The least restric-tive environments (LRE) provision of the Individuals with Disabilities Education Act (IDEA) requires that students with disabilities receive their instruction alongside their typically developing peers in general education classrooms, with the general education curriculum—unless they cannot satisfactorily meet their goals there. However, the reality of conversations surrounding placement in schools often misses the mark on the spirit of this law.

Placement decisions often hinge on the perceived learning gap between the student with a disability and grade-level expectations, rather than data showing that high-quality instruction in the general education classroom is not effective. If the student isn't on grade level or is too far away from grade level, then general education can be seen as the wrong place and unable to meet the student's needs. This way of think-ing about placement puts students into the position of needing to earn their right to be included through higher achievement—achievement that is less likely in a segregated setting. In this model of placement, stu-dents frequently end up "stuck" for years, or permanently, in segregated school settings. Our processes and thinking are in dire need of a new narrative.

In most countries, students are grouped by their age level, and curricula are devised for each year's group. However, there can be many sixth-grade classes, for example, where no students are working on the standards or curriculum for that specific year. Instead, some are below and some are above what is expected for that age group. This promotes the labeling of slow and fast learners, but this is misleading as these terms are defined by an expectation (Grade 6 performance), whereas many may be making great progress and others are not. Importantly, the myth of slow and fast learners has been repeatedly dispelled. As Koedinger et al. (2023) demonstrated, students are often at different starting points, but they all can gain the same amount of learning from the tasks and practice they complete. Based on their analysis of 7,000 students, they found no evidence that some students progressed faster than others. They did find that some students had a head start. The challenge is that teachers stop teaching when a group of students has reached mastery, leaving some behind and labeled as slow learners.

There are a few countries where curricula are not defined by year (e.g., New Zealand) but by levels, such that in Year 6, there can be students working at Level 2 up to Level 5 of the curricula (the expectation is Year 6 = Level 4), and the teacher is expected to move all students up at least a level across two years. Teachers are not seen as ineffective if students do not all reach the expectation of Year 6, but they are seen as effective when all move up at least one level. Students are not labeled slow or fast relative to the year's expectations. Educators understand that the more important metric is growth from the starting level at the beginning of the school year.

Even worse than making decisions based on performance level, IEP teams often select a more restrictive setting and justify this setting based on a label. In these cases, the assumption is that if students have a certain diagnosis or IQ score, then the general education classroom isn't appropriate. For example, some districts default to having all students identified with autism in the same program, often requiring students to be bussed across town away from their neighborhood peers to attend class. But what do we mean by appropriate? Appropriate for whom?

The student or the adults? Are the expectations relative to the year's group or the growth from the start of the year?

As we've already explored through our illustration of the jagged learner profile, a disability label actually reveals little about the individual child's specific needs. Critically important, the unlabeled student is much more successful than the labeled student ($d = -.61$; Corwin, 2024). Think about this finding: take two students of the same academic, behavioral, and/or social profile. Now label one but not the other, and the labeled student experiences a loss equivalent to 0.61 standard deviations below their peer not labeled! Why? The problem is that the labels can lead to low expectations and fewer opportunities for some students. Lower expectations held by the teacher, the student, and the system. As a consequence, expectations become reality.

We've got a long history of inventing labels and assigning students to groups. Diagnoses and labels may provide a starting point for understanding students' learning needs. But in schools, labeling too often is used to segregate students such that they receive lesser quality and quantity of instruction, which can lead to reduced cognitive challenge, lower expectations, and more tasks at the current level of performance rather than in the zone of proximal development. There is an urgent need to raise the expectations of teaching and learning for students with labels.

There are compelling reasons to ask different questions when making placement decisions. First and foremost, students with disabilities have legal and human rights to be included. Second, we have ever-growing evidence to show that students with IEPs have better outcomes when included in classrooms with students who don't have IEPs ($d = 0.52$; Corwin, 2024; see also Cole et al., 2023). Teachers and families have expressed concern over the years that inclusion holds back students who don't have learning differences. But negative impacts of inclusion on students without disabilities are a myth. Indeed, Szumski et al. (2017) report an effect size of 0.12 for students *without* a disability in classes with students with disabilities included—everyone is a winner! When we dig deeper beyond the broad effects for all students, we see incredible outcomes for students who have been identified with a learning disability—the largest group of students who have IEPs. For every core subject area that high school students with learning disabilities complete in inclusive classrooms, they are 1.6 times more likely to go on to post-secondary education (Joshi & Bouck, 2017).

From the Classroom

Impact on Classroom Teachers

Eileen was a newish teacher and was hired at a high school that educated students with significant disabilities in general classrooms. Eileen wanted to teach honors and advanced placement classes but was hired to teach ninth grade. Given the nature of the school and the automatic scheduling of students with disabilities into general classes, Jamie was enrolled in Eileen's first-period class. Eileen was provided with an infused skills grid that included a number of IEP-related goals that could be addressed in the English classroom. When talking with the advocate teacher (funded by special education and sometimes called educational specialist, special educator, or learning specialist), Eileen learned about the successful approaches used in the past to support Jamie's academic and social learning. The advocate teacher also noted that the peers in the class knew Jamie and that Eileen should ask them for advice as well.

Fast forward a semester. Jamie is successful in Eileen's class and all of the other ninth-grade classes, but equally importantly, Eileen has learned to be an even better teacher. She noted that she didn't learn about supports for students with jagged profiles when she was in school or from her teacher education program. She learned about supporting a wide range of student needs by teaching Jamie and her peers in class. And the skills Eileen developed from supporting students with disabilities in inclusive classrooms transferred to her support for other students who also had needs, some of which were not identified. From this experience, Eileen reflected that she learned about the value of peer supports. She noted that the world would be different when the students grew up because they wouldn't know any different—peers with disabilities were part of their classes and experiences. Thus, they would be more likely to advocate for people with disabilities and those who were different from themselves as adults when it came to housing, the workplace, and society. And this was in 1999.

An Infused Skills Grid

The infused skills grid (Fisher et al., 2004) is an essential tool that allows educators to align students' needs, such as those outlined in an IEP, with the routines and content of the general education curriculum. This method provides a concrete way to ensure that students with significant learning needs can fully participate in general classroom environments in meaningful ways. Many educators feel confident in differentiating instruction when students' skills are only slightly above or below the success criteria set for the class, but when there is a more significant gap—such as is often the case for students with intellectual disabilities—teachers may struggle to plan for inclusion. The infused skills grid bridges that gap, offering a structure to map out both content and skill development in a way that engages all students, regardless of their starting points.

In planning these opportunities, it is important to ensure students' participation, which is not about keeping them superficially included but about achieving measurable and meaningful progress. The grid works by cross-referencing the priority skills outlined in a student's IEP with the objectives and learning outcomes of the general education curriculum. Every activity should be linked to explicit learning outcomes that target students' development in critical areas such as literacy, numeracy, fine motor skills, and communication. This allows teams to identify opportunities for meaningful participation and skill-building across subjects, with tasks tailored to developmental levels but still tied to the core learning objectives of the classrooms. These outcomes should be flexible enough to evolve as students grow, allowing them to engage more deeply with the material over time as they progress toward the next level of understanding.

From the Classroom

Javier's Infused Skills Grid

Ms. Thompson, the eighth-grade team teacher leader, welcomed everyone to the meeting to create an infused skills grid for Javier, an eighth grader with an intellectual disability. Javier; his grandparents,

(Continued)

(Continued)

Juan and Carmen Sanchez; and the advocate (special education) teacher, Ms. Nakamura attended the meeting. "Good morning, everyone. It's great to see you, Javier, Mr. and Mrs. Sanchez." After a bit of small talk and catching up, Ms. Thompson focused everyone on the task ahead. "Let's dive into what the upcoming quarter will look like."

"In science, students will delve into the basics of physics through experiments. In math, they'll explore statistics and basic algebraic concepts. In English, we're focusing on analyzing classical literature. Social Studies will be all about the Civil Rights Movement. And in art, we're concentrating on portrait drawing and sculpting."

"Sculpting! Cool!" Javier interjected with enthusiasm.

Ms. Thompson responded, "Oh, it will be, Javier! Now, let's discuss your specific goals." Ms. Thompson looked to Ms. Nakamura.

Ms. Nakamura responded, "Alright, Javier. You're working on math operations like addition and subtraction up to two digits, measuring, reading longer sentences, the fine motor skills of writing and drawing, sharing your opinions, and using next-level vocabulary. And you've been making such great progress in every one of these areas!"

"I work really, really hard!" Javier declared, seemingly eager to take on the challenges.

Mr. Sanchez chimed in, "Yes, you do!"

"Now, let's build an infused skills grid so Javier can be engaged in every subject," Ms. Thompson suggested.

"I love it when we do this. It really gives an idea of how he participates and how it all comes together," Ms. Sanchez noted with a warm smile.

"Absolutely. And it helps the whole eighth-grade team stay on the same page and focused on his goals," Ms. Thompson added. "I've talked with the eighth-grade teachers, and we've got some great ideas for how Javier can work on his goals this quarter. We want your ideas, too." Ms. Thompson looked to Mr. and Mrs. Sanchez, then continued, "In science, Javier can measure and add ingredients for experiments to work on math skills. He can also read short experiment instructions to develop his decoding skills." Everyone nodded in agreement, and Ms. Thompson typed into a shared document.

Ms. Sanchez added, "Javier loves to help me with cooking, don't you?" Looking at an agreeable Javier, she offered, "Javier can help measure in the kitchen with me."

"That's perfect," Ms. Nakamura affirmed. "In math, he can work on addition and subtraction problems, measuring shapes, and read shortened math word problems for his sentence reading."

"For English, Javier can dictate story summaries and draw pictures with sentences to improve his fine motor and writing skills," Ms. Thompson continued.

"I can do that!" Javier assured everyone in the room.

"Excellent," Ms. Nakamura agreed. "In Social Studies, he can work on sharing his opinion related to the Civil Rights Movement and write down key historical terms. Since the whole class will be doing that, it's a good opportunity to work on a goal that everyone is learning."

Mr. Sanchez added, "Could he do it in the same way as in English, with the dictating stories with pictures so it's the same in both places?"

Everyone nodded in agreement. Ms. Nakamura affirmed, "That's a really good idea. I'll get together with both teachers to make sure this looks the same across both content areas."

"Lastly, in art, Javier can measure shapes, give his opinion on varying examples of art, and focus on fine motor skills through precision in sculpting and pencil holding for portrait drawing," Ms. Thompson concluded.

"Perfect," Ms. Nakamura affirmed. "It seems we have a solid plan for making sure Javier has the right opportunities in each of his classes this quarter."

Ms. Thompson finalized the grid, looking around the room. "Javier, are you ready?"

"Ready!" Javier confirmed.

(Continued)

(Continued)

		SUBJECT				
		SCIENCE	MATH	ELA	SOCIAL STUDIES	ART
TARGET SKILLS	Measuring	Measure experiment ingredients	Measure shapes			Measure shapes
	Adding & Subtracting	Add experiment instructions	Addition and subtraction problems, using manipulatives			Read art technique instructions
	Decoding	Read experiment instructions	Read shortened word problems	Dictate story summaries with pictures	Read short historical narratives	Read art technique instructions
	Writing & Fine Motor Skills	Write words describing his observations during experiments	Write numbers, and solve written problems	Draw illustrations for dictated stories, write words and sentences to accompany the drawings	Draw historical figures/ events, write words and sentences to accompany the drawings	Use a controlled pencil grip for portraits
	Sharing Opinions	Give opinions on experiment results		Dictate opinions on literature	Dictate opinions on civil rights issues	Critique art examples
	Using Expanded Vocabulary	Describe experiments using science vocabulary	Describe his math work using math vocabulary	Use new vocabulary words in his summaries of stories	Use civil rights vocabulary in his opinion statements	Describe art using new art vocabulary

The *least* dangerous assumption we can make about our students is that they are competent, able to learn, and will have wonderful, fulfilling lives. The *most* dangerous assumption we can make is that they should be excluded because they can't succeed. Thus, the only reason we could ever justify removal from general education classrooms is when the skills that the student needs to develop cannot be taught or practiced in those classrooms. But then we have to ask about the skills themselves. It's hard to imagine that students with disabilities need to learn skills that other students their age are not using or learning. Some of these skills may not be the focus of instruction, but other students will likely use those skills, having learned them in the past. Imagine the difference when our assumptions come true. When identifying skills, educators should ask the following:

- Are other students using or learning this skill?
- Will the student be able to use this skill on their own once mastered?
- Will the skill increase the student's autonomy?

In the past, we've seen cases made for functional "life skills" added as goals for students with low-incidence disabilities (e.g., grocery shopping as a goal for a student with significant intellectual disability). If we apply the questions above to that skill, it would be hard to justify removing a fourth grader from the classroom to practice grocery shopping because other students that age are not learning that skill in school. It's also unlikely that the student will be allowed to use that skill independently if it is learned in the next few months. However, let's say the student needs physical therapy, which could be more challenging to align with the general curriculum. In that case, we would have to determine when the student could receive this support during the school day, which may require some time outside the regular classroom. We might be able to align physical therapy with physical education time, but we also want to be careful in choosing where we select to pull. If, for example, physical education is the student's favorite time of day, or if the student can work on important motor goals during this time, it may not be the obvious choice it seems to be.

The least dangerous assumption for Javier was that he could participate and gain valuable learning in the inclusive eighth-grade classroom. As we're sure you noticed, Javier's targeted skills are not at the eighth-grade level. However, whether he could pass grade-level expectations was not the topic of conversation for his team. They presumed competence in both Javier and his eighth-grade team of teachers.

Instead of asking whether a student with a disability is "appropriate" for a general education classroom, we should ask, "Can the student gain valuable learning in this inclusive setting?" This question shifts our focus from fitting students into predetermined boxes to creating environments that nurture their growth and development. As educators, we must have high expectations for ALL students and teach them to embrace new challenges that advance their learning. Mindframe two states that all students can achieve at high levels. However, dismantling segregated structures so that more students with IEPs are fully included is the kind of change that doesn't happen overnight. It begins with seeing the moral imperative to do so and treating the need as urgent, as we would with any other equity or human rights priority.

Summary

One of the hallmarks of successful teaching and learning is great diagnosis and discovery, and most of us would want to know and understand such a diagnosis. Explaining one's learning and the chance to connect with others with the same experience can be valuable. But labeling based on such diagnosis also comes with the danger of lowered expectations and a subsequent self-fulfilling prophecy. Educators are tasked with ensuring students advance in their learning, which requires keeping the bar high and expecting the unexpected. Our students are counting on us for both.

Labels can be passports to services, but they are not the key to understanding variability. When labels lead to segregated environments or lowered expectations, they rob students of opportunity and their human rights to be included and can cause irreparable harm. The evidence suggests that when we remove a focus on these labels, students perform better. We're not suggesting that students shouldn't be diagnosed, have an IEP, and receive services. These provide legal protections that some countries are fortunate to have. However, the paradox prompts caution. Unfortunately, the document that's designed to protect can also lead to building walls that isolate, and we can't let this happen. As long as separate rooms exist for some students, they will be filled.

We owe it to our students to dig deeper and understand their individual strengths, preferences, interests, and needs. From these points of variability, we make decisions about instruction and intervention, expecting the moon. We need to make courageous decisions to expect that students can be successful in inclusive settings and design those settings for inclusion. Labels have no place in our decisions about intervention and certainly no place in forming our expectations. Labels guide us to where to look. They can direct us to the best instructional solutions, but they do not define students and what they are able to achieve. Labels, too, are a means to legal rights. Because of the role of labels in defining eligibility, some students have special rights. But all students have special needs.

Learning Check

I can describe the potential harm caused by labeling students and how it can lead to lowered expectations and segregated placements.

STRONGLY DISAGREE	DISAGREE	NEUTRAL	AGREE	STRONGLY AGREE
1	2	3	4	5

I can explain with evidence why inclusive classrooms benefit all students, including those with and without disabilities.

STRONGLY DISAGREE	DISAGREE	NEUTRAL	AGREE	STRONGLY AGREE
1	2	3	4	5

I can identify and evaluate moments when I may have allowed labels or assumptions to influence expectations and adjust my approach to be more inclusive and empowering.

STRONGLY DISAGREE	DISAGREE	NEUTRAL	AGREE	STRONGLY AGREE
1	2	3	4	5

3 Differentiation Provides Multiple Pathways to Succeed

Learning Intention

- I am learning to design and implement instructional strategies that provide multiple pathways for all students to achieve shared learning goals.

Success Criteria

- I can define differentiated instruction and describe its importance in supporting diverse student needs.
- I can identify and prioritize the essential skills and concepts my students need to learn and align them with clear success criteria.
- I can deliver differentiated instruction to meet the needs of the students I teach.
- I can analyze the impact of my differentiation strategies on student learning and make data-informed adjustments to improve outcomes.

In this book, we explore the ways that teachers think about their practice—the mindframes that can make classrooms more inclusive and teaching more flexible in response to students' jagged profiles. The chapters on Mindframes One and Two both contain examples of powerful ways of organizing and delivering instruction—for example, using Universal Design for Learning (UDL) and infused skills grids. All these approaches provide multiple pathways for students to succeed.

This is important because differentiation, or differentiated instruction, has proven to be an effective approach to teaching diverse groups of students (d = .58; Corwin, 2024). It means using a wide variety of teaching techniques, adapting lessons, providing multiple pathways to the same goal, and arranging sufficient time for students to engage successfully with learning opportunities. Carol Ann Tomlinson, a key thinker about differentiation, also suggests that it is important to consider learners' profiles, their readiness to engage with particular content, and interests when differentiating instruction (Tomlinson & Imbeau, 2023).

Although the importance of differentiation to classrooms full of diverse learners is clear, it is among education's most confused concepts. We have shared language but not a shared *understanding*. It can mean a process, a way of thinking, a set of activities, a rule for planning, or an algorithm. The aim of differentiation, however, is typically to enable all students to maximize their learning no matter where they start and at what speed they learn. The motivation for teachers to use differentiated instruction starts from worthy premises already discussed in this book: All students are unique, and diversity is the norm.

A way to unpack differentiated instruction is to begin by thinking about the impact of effective teaching on every student. All teaching, differentiated or not, should acknowledge that diversity is the reality of our classrooms. In this way, many methods commonly claimed to be related to differentiated instruction can be more simply described as excellent teaching. Tier 1 whole class instruction that is as good as it can be for all learners includes the following:

- assessing and activating prior knowledge
- the intentional and purposeful release of responsibility
- matching instruction to assessment data
- providing clear, unambiguous learning intentions
- teacher modeling

- providing multiple opportunities to learn
- continually checking for student understanding
- backward design
- guided and independent practice

When teachers think of differentiated instruction as providing multiple pathways and multiple times to succeed, they are on their way to acknowledging and addressing student heterogeneity. This mindframe is very different from the traditional grammar of schooling based on teachers delivering lessons at the front of their classes, students being compliant, working on the same tasks, and teachers attempting to reduce student variability to make their work easier. This dominant grammar is based on teachers talking (about 90 percent of the time), asking 150+ questions a day, requiring fewer-than-three-word responses from their students, and focusing on facts, facts, and more facts. Teachers assess to see that their students heard the facts, ask students to "do" activities, prescribe assignments that need to be handed in on time, and then grade and give feedback about the rightness or wrongness of the work. Students are grouped in classes of 20–40, labeled if they do not reach average performance, taught age-based curricula even though many students are not working at their age level (many above, many below), and they sit for national tests. It is no surprise that variance is the norm for these tests!

This example may seem extreme, but variations of this grammar have long dominated schooling (Cuban, 2020). It was, however, severely disrupted by COVID protocols. What a (unfortunate) natural experiment we all experienced when teaching during the COVID-19 pandemic. Teachers could not talk to students online 90 percent of the time. They had to adjust, learn how to triage, listen, and ensure students were taught to learn independently and cooperatively. The eight meta-analyses already published on the effects of COVID around the world show the overall effect size for its impact was minimal (d = about –.16, about the same decrease in achievement that many students lose over the summer break; Corwin, 2024). This low average effect associated with COVID disruption attests to the expertise and resilience of teachers in making significant adjustments in difficult circumstances

(Hattie, 2021). Given exceptional circumstances during COVID, there was much more differentiation in classrooms—more teaching of skills to facilitate students working alone and with peers, less teacher talk, more release of teacher responsibility, and more lessons that appropriately challenged all learners.

What Is Differentiation?

Differentiation has a central premise that ensures the learning goals are *not* changed. The principle is that teachers do not change the intended learning outcomes; instead, they arrange for their students to access different ways and amounts of time to succeed. Differentiation is not about assigning tasks that reduce students' learning opportunities but about empowering students to attain the success criteria set for lessons, allowing for different routes and times to success.

Once again, differentiation is *not* different activities for different groups of students. This tends to reinforce low expectations and leads to students with slower progress and lower starting points barely catching up, often widening the achievement gaps. (Note, as we say elsewhere in this book, small-group instruction is great, as long as the group isn't labeled and is never seen as even quasi-permanent).

One way of establishing differentiation as central to classroom teaching and not as an "extra" is by using UDL as a foundation for planning and lesson design. UDL has already been introduced as part of Mindframe One. It is a planning framework that focuses on making the curriculum accessible for all learners by examining at the outset the barriers that might occur in the delivery of teaching and learning activities (d =.43; Corwin, 2024). This prevents retrofitting or changing instruction at the point of delivery (Chita-Tegmark et al., 2011), which can impact teachers' confidence in delivering teaching and learning activities to diverse learners. Although UDL was originally developed for learners with disabilities, recent meta-analyses suggest it is effective for all learners and useful across all school settings (Capp, 2017; King-Sears et al., 2023).

Table 3.1, adapted from Berman et al. (2024), highlights some key differences between the traditional format and structure of schooling and UDL-informed instruction. UDL aims to accommodate all learners through flexible instructional practice and assessment. This includes being adaptable when delivering content, drawing on students' strengths and interests, encouraging active learning, and ensuring that assessments are varied and target the skills and knowledge taught.

TABLE 3.1 Comparing Traditional and UDL Instruction

TRADITIONAL INSTRUCTION	UNIVERSALLY DESIGNED INSTRUCTION
• Teachers typically deliver content one way. • Students are passive learners who acquire information through memorizing, practicing, and taking tests. • The learning environment encourages students to sit quietly and work on identical tasks. • Students' skills and knowledge of content are assessed using one method.	• Teachers deliver content in multiple ways. • Students are active learners who engage with and analyze the content to gain understanding by themselves and through collaborating with others. • The learning environment encourages students to explore content based on personal interests, preferences, and abilities. • Students are allowed to demonstrate their skills and knowledge of content using one of several methods.

Note: Adapted from Berman et al. (2024).

But UDL is much more than a table of strategies. Implementing the essential core of UDL requires thinking like a universal designer who anticipates barriers and designs instruction with predictable variability and known barriers in mind. Such thinking keeps the jagged profiles of all learners at the forefront, right from the beginning, before teachers are even familiar with the specific learning needs of all their students. UDL is a way of designing instruction ahead of time. In fact, the more we design universally, the less differentiation we have to do because we've already planned for variation.

From the Classroom

Keeping the Goal in Sight

Mr. Parker's eighth-grade history class was working on a hands-on project about ancient civilizations. The assignment was straightforward: Students would work in groups to create a diorama of a chosen civilization, illustrating key aspects of its culture, architecture, and daily life. The project was meant to be a creative way for students to demonstrate their understanding of the content.

However, Mr. Parker had a few students who struggled with reading comprehension and attention, and he wanted to make sure they could participate. To differentiate, he gave those students a simpler version of the project. Instead of researching and presenting detailed information about their civilization's economy, political systems, and innovations, they focused solely on building the physical diorama. Mr. Parker thought this would ensure that everyone could stay engaged and contribute.

The classroom was filled with the energy of students cutting, gluing, and discussing their projects during class. Each group was hard at work, building models of temples, market squares, and homes. The students who had the simplified version of the task, including Kayla and James, were busy, too—cutting out pieces of cardboard and gluing them together. But Mr. Parker noticed something. While most students discussed the significance of the structures they were building, Kayla and James's group wasn't engaging with the historical content. They were absorbed in the construction but had little understanding of how their diorama connected to the civilization they were supposed to be learning about.

After the presentations, it became clear that Kayla and James hadn't gained the same depth of understanding as their peers. Although their diorama looked impressive, they struggled to answer questions about the civilization's key achievements or how the diorama's architecture reflected culture. Their project had been hands-on, like everyone else's, but the learning outcomes were too shallow. Mr. Parker realized that by lowering the expectations for their contribution, he had missed an opportunity to help Kayla and James engage with historical concepts.

Reflecting on this, Mr. Parker saw that although the hands-on activity was engaging, it wasn't enough to simplify by making tasks "easier" for some students. This wasn't differentiation at all. What Kayla and James needed wasn't a simpler project but more scaffolding to help them understand and present the historical content that was the focus of the lesson. Instead of just focusing on the construction, Mr. Parker could have provided guided questions, graphic organizers, and sentence starters to help his students connect the diorama to the civilization's cultural and historical context. Kayla and James could still participate in the building activity, but with structured support, they would be pushed to engage with the core learning objectives of the lesson—just like everyone else.

The next time Mr. Parker assigned a project, he approached differentiation differently. All students would still work on hands-on tasks, but instead of simplifying the criteria for some, he provided additional support to make sure everyone could reach the same learning goals. For students like Kayla and James, this meant giving them tools to help organize their thoughts and express their understandings rather than giving them an easier version of the task.

In this way, Mr. Parker ensured that all students, regardless of their skill levels, were learning the same important content—and that no one was just "busy" on work that didn't actually deepen their understanding.

Mr. Parker's experience reminds us that we need to be very clear about what we want our students to learn from our teaching and to think carefully about whether a range of learning outcomes is appropriate. It is always important that intended learning outcomes are focused, explicit, and able to be extended as students become ready for the next level of depth of understanding.

A central aspect of differentiation is variation in the intensity of teaching depending on students' needs. Educators who adopt the mindframes outlined in this book have already considered the jagged profiles their students have and used a UDL approach in the construction of learning environments and tasks. In addition, these educators consider the needs of their students to identify any additional differentiation necessary. The kinds of deliberate changes that teachers make to the intensity of their teaching in response to information about student learning are described in Table 3.2 (adapted from Berman et al., 2024).

TABLE 3.2 Changes in Intensity of Teaching

INTENSITY AS . . .	APPROPRIATE WHEN . . .
Repeated learning experiences	• a skill is not yet consistently demonstrated, and more opportunities to consolidate learning are needed • a skill is established, and it is useful for that skill to become more fluent • specific concepts or vocabulary need to become established and remembered • students have an intellectual disability, specific cognitive difficulty, or other condition that means more practice is needed for the skill or understanding to be established
Increasingly explicit content, monitoring, and feedback	• delayed responsiveness to teaching may be because of misconceptions, partial learning, or skills that are developing
Smaller learning group	• teachers need to focus closely on their students as learners; the smaller the group the more intense the focus, and the more direct the teaching and assessment
More frequent opportunities and varied length of activities	• more frequent opportunities are needed; shorter intense periods of teaching are accessed more easily than longer sessions; alternately longer periods of instruction allow for depth of learning
Increasing challenge	• students need to develop more depth of learning or extension of skills, or require opportunities to apply knowledge or skills
Access to specialist expertise	• it is determined that specialist assessment of learning needs and/or access to specialist intervention is needed; a student becomes the focus of educational casework

Note: Adapted from Berman et al. (2024).

As Table 3.2 indicates, there are times when teachers make decisions about whether more of the same learning activities, practice, or a repetition of learning opportunities are needed for learners to progress or whether it is time to change the approach based on the impact that the strategies and practices have had. This may be appropriate for students who are responding to teaching less quickly than might be anticipated or than other students, or when students understand part of what is being taught, but not all of it. All of us know that we engage in learning differently if we are familiar with the content and activities compared to when we are not. Another key component of decision-making about the intensity of teaching is the degree of explicitness required to teach the content and provide feedback. Some learners will recognize connections within content, while others will need to be provided with each part of the learning content and then scaffolded to put their understandings together as a whole (Berman et al., 2024).

Differentiation Starts With Expectations

Christine Rubie-Davies (2015) argues that teachers with high expectations tend to have them for all students, with consequential high impact on students (d = .96). Sadly, teachers with low expectations tend to have them for all students and have a low impact on students (d = .02). Indeed, Rubie-Davies found that the effect size for student achievement of the teachers with high expectations was .50 to 1.44 but only .03 to .20 for teachers with low expectations. Students in classes taught by teachers with high expectations make much greater academic progress than students whose teachers have low expectations of them. High-expectation teachers tend to think of themselves as change agents and not facilitators, have growth not fixed notions of ability, are more mastery than performance goal–oriented, use a better balance of open and closed questions in their instruction, and focus more on learning rather than "doing" activities.

What was most surprising from Rubie-Davies's work is that high-expectation teachers rarely mentioned differentiation, though it was cited frequently by the teachers with low expectations. When interviewed, the high-expectation teachers argued that although they recognized students started at different points, they aimed for all students to attain the success criteria of their lessons, and, to them, differentiation meant providing different ways of attaining that success. In contrast, the low-expectation teachers defined differentiation in terms of grouping, different activities, different levels of challenge, and different opportunities. We should be wary of teachers who see differentiation as primarily a method of grouping or as involving different activities and assignments for different groups of students. This caution should seriously bring into question the use of within-class grouping where different groups are assigned work relative to their current abilities.

Rubie-Davies and Hattie (2025) showed the remarkable differences in classrooms between teachers with low and high expectations. These are dramatic differences primarily as a function of how the teacher thinks. It should be obvious which classes thrive, generate a sense of belonging and invitation to learn, and which we wish our children to be in (see Table 3.3).

TABLE 3.3 Results of Differences in Teachers' Expectations

LOW EXPECTATION	HIGH EXPECTATION
EFFECTS = -.03 TO .20	EFFECTS = .50 TO 1.44*
Expects and looks for low performance, which reinforces their views about low performance	Expects improvement, sees the errors, and seeks evidence to enact improvement
Sees greater differences between students in class	Sees fewer differences between students in class
Argues that some are expected to improve	Argues that all are expected to improve
Considers differentiation means different activities for different groups of students	Considers differentiation as different times and different ways to attain the success criteria
Has more differentiated activities in class	Has fewer differentiated activities in class
Uses ability groups and designs different activities for each group	Works with all students in mixed and flexible groups
Places students in fairly inflexible ability groups	Mainly uses interest-based grouping when needed
Comments on low effort, class behavior, poor in-class relationships	Comments on developing confidence, motivation, persistence, and attitude to work
Constantly reminds students of procedures and routines	Has procedures in place that students manage themselves
A focus on activities and behaviors	A focus on learning
Spends more time with those not performing well and asks those who are performing above expectations to work independently	Works with all equally
Communicates details of the activities to be completed	Communicates learning intentions and success criteria to the class
Asks mostly closed questions of select students	Asks more open-impact questions of all students

LOW EXPECTATION	HIGH EXPECTATION
EFFECTS = -.03 TO .20	EFFECTS = .50 TO 1.44*
Provides liberal praise	Provides primarily "where to next" feedback
Makes many negative statements about learning and behavior	Makes many positive statements about learning and creates high trust
Provides lots of repetition and lower-level activities for lower achievers and high level for high-achieving students	Engages all in advanced, challenging activities
Little use of student prior knowledge	More often uses students' prior knowledge to make connections

Students *know* why they are assigned to different groups, despite our creativity at naming and disguising the reasons. Indeed, the effect size of student expectations is very high ($d = 1.23$; Corwin, 2024) and even more influential than teachers' expectations. Putting the two together, the effects can be accelerating or toxic. Students know about their teachers' expectations, feel it as part of their groupings within the class, and soon know their place in the school's learning environment. The teacher's role is to help students exceed beyond what they think they can achieve, create opportunities for all to flourish, and to provide alternatives to mundane or repetitive activities that maintain instead of raise students' levels of achievement. All students need to be given the chance to accelerate their learning.

Differentiation requires that teachers and students maintain high expectations for all students. Differentiation sets the conditions that accelerate students' learning and enable them to succeed in different ways and at different times. The goal is for all students to be empowered to attain the success criteria of the lessons. How do you balance high expectations with the need for individualized support in your classroom?

____

____

____

____

Differentiation Requires Intentional Instruction

Explicit, systematic teaching is central to effective teaching (Hattie, 2023) and is vital for many students, for example, those who may not develop most skills without it (Hempenstall, 2020). Explicit teaching depends on the following:

- having structured lessons with clear goals
- including planning for multiple exposures and practice opportunities, such as worked examples
- supporting learning through expert questioning and task-related feedback (Berman et al., 2024)

Explicit teaching also requires a gradual release of responsibility to the student (e.g., Fisher & Frey, 2021), working with students to self-assess their progress, and ensuring that they are using the optimal learning strategies aligned to each task's demands. These are all components of expert lesson planning and represent core competencies for teachers.

Small group learning is one way to increase the intensity of teaching. This flexible arrangement allows teachers to target students who need explicit teaching and provide them with more opportunities for practice or, alternatively, a different concentration of time on aspects of learning. Small group instruction should supplement the quality whole-class instruction that is vital for all students to receive. Small group instruction allows for acceleration of learning, but teachers will run out of time if they try to teach everything in small groups.

The smallest group, and therefore the most intense, is when one teacher works with one student. This can be appropriate at times and may be the most effective way for teachers to provide what is needed. One-on-one interactions mean identified teaching needs can be acted upon immediately. As this is logistically difficult, a compromise is to organize and reorganize students into learning groups flexibly. If students become accustomed to being grouped differently for various activities, this can become a routine and an effective way to adjust instruction (Berman et al., 2024). One of the keys, however, is to form groups based on specific needs and ensure there is no permanency, labeling, or lesser difficulty or depth of learning inherent in the organization of the students. Grouping is one way to allow for different emphases, different teaching methods, and different experiences—but *not* different (lower) expectations, success criteria, or demands, as Mr. Parker discovered.

Differentiation Is Not a Set of Activities

Problematic definitions of differentiated instruction (Dack, 2019) include the ideas that differentiation is

- merely a set of strategies or activities,
- only pertinent for struggling or advanced learners,
- about different goals for different learners, and
- the provision of individualized instruction.

These four ideas are barriers to the effective use of differentiated instruction because they take the teacher back to the notion of teaching to the middle of a class, with extensions for faster or slower learners, or the use of additional or different activities for those students who experience difficulty or need acceleration.

Many authors, like Schwab and Woltran (2023), have argued that differentiated instruction includes a wide collection of different didactic approaches by which "teachers proactively plan to match instruction, activities, and resources to the diverse needs of the students in their classes" (Scarparolo & MacKinnon, 2022, p. 6). Pozas and Schneider (2019, p. 74) similarly defined differentiation as "any instructional practice that enables teachers to address student heterogeneity adequately and thereby support student learning." This notion seems dominant in textbooks, teacher education programs, and so much of the literature. We disagree.

There are three problems with seeing differentiated instruction as a set of activities. First, the range of suggested activities is vast and may be applied successfully with all students. In this way, instructional success depends almost entirely on the skills and expertise of teachers to implement activities well at the right time in the learning cycle and to evaluate the impact of their teaching on their students—and switch to other strategies if those chosen first don't work. According to this way of thinking, there is no need for a concept of differentiated instruction if the meaning is based only on sets of activities. Second, there is an implicit (and, in some writing, explicit) assumption that direct teaching to the whole class is not part of differentiated instruction, when indeed it can be. Third, some teaching approaches are more aligned with teaching facts, content, and the "knowing that," while others are more aligned with relating ideas, deeper conceptual thinking, and transfer. Students need both approaches, not either. Hence, teaching strategies can differ in their effectiveness depending on where they fit in students' learning cycles; there is no one set of strategies optimal for both these important instructional purposes (Hattie, 2023).

Differentiation Focuses on Time and Pathways

Consider a GPS. It does not care where you start but wants to know where you want to end up. It then calculates the optimal route from where you began to your destination—"optimal" is usually the fastest route, but you could choose the route with the fewest highways and traffic lights, meander through villages, and take side trips. No one route is the only one; there are multiple on-ramps and many possible off-ramps. The GPS does not discipline you for not following the recommended route. It allows you to stop for lunch, visit the beach, and have ice cream. Too often, progression in school is designated as the "right way"—the way prescribed in curriculum documents (usually devoid of any evidence that this is how students progress). With this orientation, students are seen as lesser if they do not speed along the "superhighway" as outlined. The essence of differentiated instruction relates to seeing progression in learning akin to being guided by a GPS. Different times and pathways can lead to successful learning and outcomes.

Tomlinson (2017) described differentiated instruction as *student-aware teaching*, whereby teachers vigilantly monitor students' proximity to lesson goals throughout a learning cycle. The teachers then modify their teaching plans to allow multiple ways and amounts of time for students to reach the success criteria and, in so doing, enhance student efficacy and their ownership of learning. This involves teachers developing skills to anticipate roadblocks, cul de sacs, and students going down pathways in different directions. Hence, it is important to realize that there are multiple pathways to progress to success. Such complexity requires that teachers have a deep understanding of the curricula and know how to advance learning in multiple ways from "knowing that" to "knowing how" to "knowing with" and can detect where students are located on their roads to success and help them focus optimally on what comes next.

From the Classroom

Multiple Paths, Same Destination

In Ms. Jackson's seventh-grade science class, the unit on ecosystems was in full swing. Her goal was for students to understand the interdependent relationships between organisms and their environments, with each student working toward the same success criteria. Some students, like Ethan and Sarah, were soaring through the content, eager to apply complex ecological concepts. Others, like Max and Olivia, needed more time to fully grasp the foundational ideas of food chains and biodiversity.

Instead of assigning the same task to everyone and differentiating by adding "extra" work for those who finished early or simplifying activities for those who needed support, Ms. Jackson took a different approach. She thought of her students' learning paths like a GPS. Each student had the same destination—the success criteria related to ecosystems—but the routes to get there varied.

For students like Ethan and Sarah, the GPS pointed them toward projects that allowed them to explore more complex ecological interactions, such as creating food webs that incorporated their knowledge of human impact on ecosystems. They were encouraged to engage with online simulations of ecosystems, analyze data, and make predictions about how environmental changes could disrupt balance.

Max and Olivia, on the other hand, were on a different route, still focused on foundational learning through hands-on exploration. Their GPSs had them working with manipulatives, such as building physical models of simple food chains using animal figurines and string to connect predator-prey relationships visually. Ms. Jackson provided scaffolded support like sentence starters and guiding questions to ensure they weren't just "on task" but actively building toward the same learning objectives.

(Continued)

(Continued)

Throughout the unit, Ms. Jackson played the role of the GPS, monitoring student progress and adapting instruction as needed. If a student veered off course, much like a GPS recalculates the route, Ms. Jackson would adjust her teaching strategy to provide a more direct path to the success criteria, whether that meant more practice, additional resources, or deeper challenges.

By the end of the unit, every student had arrived at the destination—understanding ecosystems—but they had taken different paths to get there. Some, like Ethan, had made side trips, investigating the impact of invasive species in local ecosystems, while others, like Max, had stuck to the main roads, building a firm understanding of basic ecological relationships. In every case, Ms. Jackson ensured that all students had the opportunity to meet the success criteria in a way that made sense for them without feeling rushed or held back.

Thus, in Ms. Jackson's class, differentiated instruction worked like a well-functioning GPS: It guided students through multiple pathways, recalculating as needed and ensuring that everyone reached their learning destination successfully, no matter how they traveled.

Differentiation Is Not Tracking

There have been fourteen meta-analyses on tracking or streaming, with an overall effect size of .09, which is tiny compared to other interventions. These very low effects do not vary for what is often termed, in this tracking literature, high- (.06), medium- (–.04), or low-ability (.03) students (Steenbergen-Hu et al., 2016). Nevertheless, differentiating classes by ability grouping remains popular worldwide, especially for mathematics classes. The overall effects of tracking on mathematics and reading achievement are similarly low (reading: d = 0.00, mathematics: d = 0.02; Corwin, 2024). In addition, Castejón and Zancajo (2015) found a negative relationship between student motivation levels and the degree to which systems sort and group students into ability groups. So why do we persist with a failed intervention? Who benefits? Not the students.

The most influential in-depth study of teaching and learning in tracked classes, conducted by Oakes (2005), found that many low-track classes are deadening and non-educational environments that limit students' schooling opportunities, achievements, and life chances. When tracked, the group effects of peers working together can reinforce lower performance levels (Thrupp et al., 2002). Shanker (1993, p. 24) concluded that "kids in these [lower] tracks often get little worthwhile work to do; they spend a lot of time filling in the blanks in workbooks or ditto sheets. And because we expect almost nothing of them, they learn very little."

The research that follows shows that the effects of tracking on equity outcomes are even more profound and damaging. Oakes and Wells (1996) claimed that tracking guarantees the unfair distribution of privilege, with white and wealthy students benefiting from access to high-status knowledge that low-income students and students of color are denied. Oakes et al. (1990) found that minority students were seven times more likely to be identified as low-ability than high-ability students (see also Domina et al., 2019; Darling-Hammond, 2015; Ngo & Velasquez, 2023). Braddock (1990) also found that schools with more than 20 percent of their enrolments from minority groups were more likely to track than those with fewer minority students. Modica (2015) noted that academic tracking strengthened racial boundary-keeping and reinforced the idea among students that whiteness and academic success are correlated in a fixed way. Datnow and Park (2018) concluded that "problematic practices of tracking and ability grouping with long-term consequences continue to abound in schools and are legitimated with data. In fact, tracking remains one of the most enduring practices in American high schools, despite a robust research base denouncing it" (p. 148).

Let us seriously stop tracking: no student is the winner. Therefore, differentiation should not lead to tracking, with its invidious equity consequences and little to no effect on achievement. Instead, variance should be welcomed and seen as an opportunity for more effective teaching and learning in every classroom. How is the variance of student achievement welcomed in your classroom? In your school?

____

____

____

____

Personalization and Individualization Are Not the Essence of Differentiation

Whenever differentiation is mentioned, there is a sense that it requires teaching plans that are unique to each student. But strategies based on individualization or personalization have relatively low effects (12 meta-analyses, 793 studies, d = .24). Cooperative learning (d =.45) is more effective than individualized learning, hands down. More specifically, there are five meta-analyses on cooperative learning compared to individual learning based on 959 studies with an effect size of .55, in favor of cooperative learning (Corwin, 2024). One of the fallacies of differentiation is that teachers need separate plans, activities, or learning progressions for everyone. This is beyond the capacity of most teachers in most classrooms to devise, let alone execute. Students learn in and from groups of peers by hearing others talk about their thinking and learning strategies. They learn from how others make and correct mistakes and work together to connect and build associations between ideas.

There remains, however, the importance of focusing on the centrality of each student. Such centrality requires building all individual students' learning skills: their "I" and "we" skills when working with others; their ways of mapping their progress and success; understanding their own skills, wills, and thrills (motivations) to learn; and knowing how, when, and with whom they should work to resolve learning issues. For example, when students (e.g., in low-track classes) are deprived of hearing and working with others, when one person dominates the group, and when students (e.g., in high-track classes) do not learn to empathize and understand why others may get problems incorrect and not know how to work through their mistakes, all students are losers.

From the Classroom

Stronger Together

In Ms. Taylor's eighth-grade math class, the students were about to dive into a challenging unit on algebraic equations. Some teachers might divide students by ability, but Ms. Taylor knew the dangers of tracking and wanted to take a different approach. Instead of grouping students by skill level, she decided to maximize the variance among them by encouraging cooperative learning, allowing each student to contribute and grow.

To start, Ms. Taylor formed mixed-ability groups. In one group, Noah, a student who excelled in math, was paired with Ava, who struggled with confidence in solving equations, and Elijah, who was quick to understand concepts but sometimes rushed through problems. Another group included Maya, who was naturally strong in logic, alongside Jayden, who had great potential but often needed more time to process new material.

The task Ms. Taylor gave them was challenging: Each group had to solve multi-step algebraic equations, but they also had to explain their reasoning as they worked through the problems. It wasn't enough to find the correct answer; they had to help each other understand why certain steps were necessary.

Noah quickly solved one of the equations but realized that Ava was stuck on understanding why they needed to isolate the variable first. Instead of giving her the answer, Noah walked her through the steps, asking, "Why do you think we need to get rid of this number on the left side first?" This questioning helped Ava think critically about the problem, and by explaining it, Noah solidified his own understanding.

Meanwhile, Maya noticed that Jayden was hesitating to contribute, so she asked him directly, "What do you think the next step is?" Jayden slowly suggested, "I think we subtract from both sides?" Maya nodded, "Exactly! Why do you think that's the right move?" Jayden's confidence grew as he realized he understood more than he initially thought. By articulating his reasoning, he became more involved in the group's work.

Elijah, known for racing through problems, found himself slowing down to help his teammates, particularly when Maya asked for clarification on how he arrived at certain answers. This reflective practice deepened Elijah's learning as he had to explain not just the "how" but the "why" behind his solutions.

As the unit progressed, Ms. Taylor noticed how much the students were learning from one another. Those who initially struggled with algebra, like Ava and Jayden, gained confidence and developed problem-solving strategies, while stronger students like Noah and

(Continued)

(Continued)

Maya became better at explaining their thinking. By working in diverse groups, the students didn't focus only on their own learning—they actively contributed to the success of their peers.

The collaborative nature of the tasks ensured that no student was left behind, and everyone's voice was valued. Differentiation in Ms. Taylor's classroom wasn't about assigning different tasks based on ability; it was about leveraging each student's strengths and creating an environment where they could all support and challenge one another.

By the end of the unit, not only had every student improved their algebra skills, but they had also developed essential collaboration and communication abilities. Ms. Taylor's approach showed that, when students work together with respect for each other's contributions, the learning outcomes are far greater than when they are separated by perceived ability.

Summary

Classrooms are places where variation is the norm. Students span the range of demographic and learning profiles. Thus, differentiated instruction needs to be a major principle underpinning all teaching. Educators have looked for ways to reduce diversity among their students, but homogeneity can no longer be considered the norm. So, instead, let's embrace learning diversity! Importantly, the design of learning experiences needs to begin with UDL, such that the assets and needs of students are considered in advance of planning. This reduces the need for further differentiation but does not replace it. There will be students, especially those with complex needs, who require differentiated instruction. However, differentiation should not be used as an excuse to expect less from students or to track them into groups. In addition, differentiation is more than a series of activities or tasks that are assigned to different students based on the perception of their abilities. Quality differentiation allows teachers to know where their students currently are, in terms of assets and skills, and then to design learning so that no matter where they start, students make at least a year's progress for a year's input. To do so, teachers need to be adaptive and evaluative, have multiple strategies, know when to use these strategies, be clear about how success looks, and always attend to their impact on student learning.

Learning Check

I can define differentiated instruction and describe its importance in supporting diverse student needs.

STRONGLY DISAGREE	DISAGREE	NEUTRAL	AGREE	STRONGLY AGREE
1	2	3	4	5

I can identify and prioritize the essential skills and concepts my students need to learn and align them with clear success criteria.

STRONGLY DISAGREE	DISAGREE	NEUTRAL	AGREE	STRONGLY AGREE
1	2	3	4	5

I can deliver differentiated instruction to meet the needs of the students I teach.

STRONGLY DISAGREE	DISAGREE	NEUTRAL	AGREE	STRONGLY AGREE
1	2	3	4	5

I can analyze the impact of my differentiation strategies on student learning and make data-informed adjustments to improve outcomes.

STRONGLY DISAGREE	DISAGREE	NEUTRAL	AGREE	STRONGLY AGREE
1	2	3	4	5

4 Instruction Can Prevent Gaps and Intervention Can Close Them

Learning Intention

- I am learning about an integrated multi-tiered system of support (MTSS) as a framework for making decisions about instruction and intervention.

Success Criteria

- I can describe the three tiers of MTSS, including their purposes and implementation.
- I can dispel common misunderstandings about the MTSS framework.
- I can connect my understanding of MTSS to the broader concepts of universal design, differentiation, and data-driven decision-making, to create a cohesive and responsive instructional framework.

So far, we've focused on whole-classroom strategies, emphasizing the importance of creating environments that are inclusive and responsive to the diverse needs of all students. This universal approach is the foundation for building effective, welcoming classrooms that address a wide range of needs. However, universally designed practices alone aren't enough to meet the full spectrum of student needs. Some students will require additional support, and this group includes more than just those with Individualized Education Programs (IEPs). The presence of an IEP doesn't determine the need for intervention. Remember those false dichotomies? A student's need for intervention is dictated by their learning needs, not by their paperwork.

When students need more support beyond what's provided in the classroom, even with solid UDL and differentiation practices in place, key questions arise:

- How do we determine who needs intervention?
- How much intervention is necessary?
- What does this support look like?
- Is support provided within the classroom or in a separate setting?
- Who will deliver intervention?

Using integrated Multi-Tiered Systems of Support (MTSS) answers these questions and provides a fluid structure for students to receive excellent classroom instruction *and* intervention when needed. MTSS is a powerful tool with a proven ability to improve learning outcomes (d = .81; Corwin, 2024) and is often represented as a pyramid with three tiers: Tier 1 is the core classroom instruction for all students, Tier 2 is targeted intervention for some students, and Tier 3 is intensive intervention for a few students (see Figure 4.1).

MTSS isn't an intervention or a particular practice but a framework for making decisions about instruction and intervention. Logically, MTSS has a high effect size because it packages high-leverage influences in classroom teaching, targeted interventions, and data-driven decision-making. Although MTSS is widely regarded as a powerful tool for improving learning outcomes, inadequate implementation often holds schools back from fully realizing its benefits. The following are the six most common misunderstandings we see in schools.

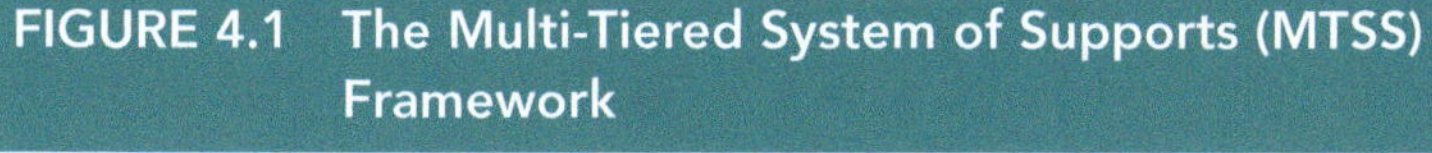
FIGURE 4.1 The Multi-Tiered System of Supports (MTSS) Framework

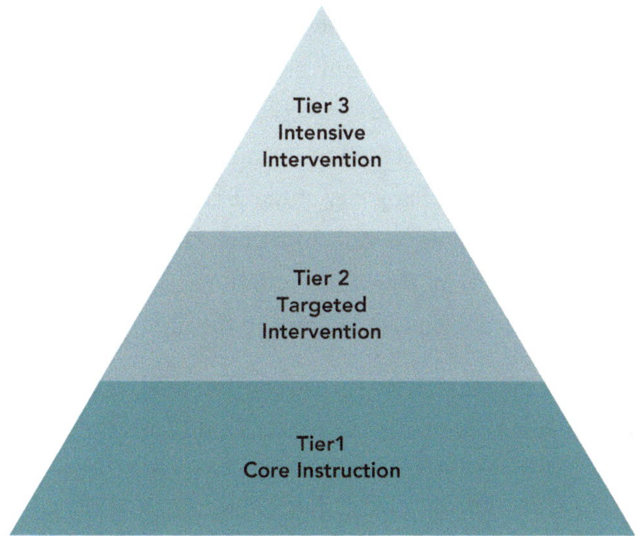

Misunderstanding 1: MTSS is about intervention.

Reality: MTSS is not solely an intervention model; it is fundamentally a prevention model.

A common misconception is that the purpose of MTSS is to identify students with significant learning gaps and funnel them into targeted interventions to help them catch up. Although intervention is essential to MTSS, this perspective misses its primary focus: prevention. MTSS is designed to address potential risks early before they grow into significant gaps. As Benjamin Franklin wisely observed, "An ounce of prevention is worth a pound of cure," and this principle is at the heart of MTSS.

Prevention begins with excellent, research-based core instruction designed to serve all students. The goal is to ensure that the majority of students succeed through this instruction without requiring additional interventions.

Consider reading instruction as an example. In some schools, explicit phonics instruction is offered only to students identified as struggling, typically through small-group pullouts or targeted interventions.

Although this may help those students in the short term, it does not address the systemic issue: a lack of high-quality instruction for all students. Research clearly shows that explicit phonics instruction benefits all students—not just those with decoding difficulties. It's also most effective when delivered universally at the outset, rather than as a reactive measure after less effective instruction has failed some students. In MTSS, this instruction is embedded universally into the core reading block, ensuring every student can access evidence-based practices. When instruction is delivered universally, the number of students requiring Tier 2 or Tier 3 interventions decreases significantly because fewer students experience gaps in the first place.

Effective Tier 1 instruction relies on continuously reviewing data to refine and enhance core teaching practices proactively. Teachers use formative assessments and classroom data to identify patterns of need and adjust their instruction accordingly. For example, suppose classroom assessments reveal that students in a third-grade classroom are struggling with multi-step problem-solving. In that case, the teacher might incorporate additional modeling and guided practice into lessons for the entire class. This "instructional agility" ensures we address potential gaps in instruction before they grow into gaps in learning, reducing the need for intensive interventions later.

Another key feature of Tier 1 instruction is using universal screeners to identify potential needs at the very first sign. Screeners, typically administered three times a year, are intentionally designed to overidentify risk so that no need is overlooked. For example, a screener might flag a first grader who is showing early signs of difficulty with phonemic awareness. Rather than waiting for that student to fall significantly behind their peers, intervention happens immediately, addressing the need and closing the gap before it widens.

MTSS is not "business as usual." The very nature of the framework is to question every aspect of core instruction and answer those questions with data—both from research and classroom assessments. Strong Tier 1 practices focus on providing all students with high-leverage, evidence-based instruction from the start. Think of Tier 1 as the foundation of a house. Without a strong foundation, the structure above it falters. Similarly, if Tier 1 is weak, the entire MTSS framework becomes reactive rather than proactive, relying too heavily on interventions. We can see we have effective core instruction when 80–90 percent of students progress well without additional support. By focusing on prevention and dynamic instruction, MTSS creates a system where students stay on track, reducing the likelihood of large gaps and intensive interventions down the road (McIntosh & Goodman, 2016).

Misunderstanding 2: Tier 2 is for students who need support but don't have an IEP.

Reality: Tier 2 interventions are for any student who needs targeted support, regardless of whether they have an IEP.

A second misconception is that the MTSS tiers can be sorted into categories based on labels: Tier 1 is for students who don't need extra support, Tier 2 is for those who need intervention but don't qualify for an IEP, and Tier 3 is for students who have or need an IEP. This oversimplification suggests that MTSS operates in parallel to special education, with one system serving students without IEPs and the other reserved for those with IEPs. In reality, MTSS was designed as a unified framework to address the needs of all students, regardless of labels.

Tier 2 interventions are research-based supports, targeting critical skills, usually delivered two to three times per week for at least thirty minutes and persisting for a planned period of time, usually six- to eight-week cycles. And whoever demonstrates a need for this skill is in this intervention cycle, whether or not they have an IEP. For example, a student with an IEP and a learning disability might need targeted number sense intervention. A student without an IEP may be in the same intervention group because assessment data reveal a similar need. Both students work together toward the same skill-based goals because the grouping is determined by shared needs, not labels (McIntosh & Goodman, 2016).

This integrated approach ensures that students with and without IEPs benefit from the same data-driven process. Students who need math interventions get math interventions; students who need regulation support receive regulation support, diagnosis or no diagnosis. Grouping students by shared needs, rather than shared eligibility status, also increases the efficiency and effectiveness of Tier 2 interventions—and the entire system. It avoids the pitfall of creating separate systems for students with and without IEPs and instead centers interventions on evidence-based strategies that work for everyone. MTSS eliminates the arbitrary distinctions between general education and special education supports, allowing schools to focus on meeting the specific needs of students.

Misunderstanding 3: Tier 3 is special education.

Reality: Tier 3 is an intensive intervention for any student.

A third mistaken belief about MTSS is that Tier 3 is exclusively for students who qualify for special education, which then creates unnecessary barriers to intensive support for students who need it but don't have IEPs. This misunderstanding reflects the incorrect assumption that students with IEPs have the most intensive needs. At any given time, the student in the building with the needs for the most support is likely to be a student without an IEP.

Tier 3 represents the most intensive level of intervention and is delivered based on individual student needs and their response to previous supports. As with Tier 2, Tier 3 intervention is not linked to IEP eligibility. Many students who receive Tier 3 interventions don't have IEPs. For instance, a student who received poor early reading instruction might fall significantly behind in reading fluency. This student would likely make significant gains with daily, small-group phonics instruction (Tier 3 intervention), even though they don't have a learning disability or qualify for special education.

Schools that see Tier 3 as special education risk underserving and overidentifying these students. Students who don't qualify for special education can miss out on the intensive interventions they need. And students with academic needs can be identified as having a disability, even if their needs are entirely due to poor instruction. Intensive intervention aims to close the gaps in critical skills as quickly as possible. Once mastery is achieved, the intervention is discontinued. By focusing on skills rather than labels, MTSS ensures that interventions are delivered as intensely as needed, for as long as needed—but no longer.

By ensuring that Tier 3 interventions are available to all students based on need, MTSS protects against inequities in both underserving and overidentification. Whether a student has an IEP or not, the decision to provide Tier 3 support is based solely on the data and the student's response to instruction and intervention. MTSS creates a flexible, equitable system where the most intensive interventions are accessible to anyone who needs them.

Misunderstanding 4: MTSS delays special education referral.

Reality: MTSS provides the clarity to make (or not make) a diagnosis.

One of the most persistent misunderstandings about MTSS is that it delays identifying students for special education evaluations, particularly for those who may have a specific learning disability. This concern stems from the misunderstanding that schools must "go through" MTSS before initiating a special education evaluation. In reality, MTSS is not a barrier to diagnosis; it is a process that provides critical context for understanding the root causes of a student's difficulties.

The 2004 reauthorization of the Individuals with Disabilities Education Act (IDEA) brought significant changes to how "specific learning disability" is identified, precisely to address the problem of overidentification. Before 2004, most students who qualified for an IEP in the category of specific learning disability did so based on a discrepancy between their IQ score and academic performance. But the poor performance of many of these students was not due to a neurological difference; rather, it was due to suboptimal instruction. IDEA 2004 removed the requirement to use the discrepancy model and allowed schools to use MTSS as a means of determining whether a student's difficulties were due to insufficient instruction or a true learning disability.

MTSS plays a necessary role in the referral process by ensuring that we rule out inadequate instruction as the root cause of the challenges a student is experiencing. If a student continues to struggle despite cycles of intensive interventions, the evidence of a neurological explanation is stronger. For example, a fourth-grade student struggling with reading fluency might begin receiving Tier 2 interventions focused on phonics and decoding. Through progress monitoring, the team sees that the student is not making sufficient progress, even when interventions are intensified. These data strengthen the case for a specific learning disability evaluation, as it demonstrates that the student's challenges persist despite receiving excellent instruction and intensive support.

By ensuring that students are not referred for special education prematurely, MTSS prevents overidentification of learning disability (Fuchs & Fuchs, 2006). At the same time, it reduces the likelihood of under-identification by gathering robust data to support evaluations when they are necessary. What's important is that this process does not delay *intervention*. When students are suspected of having a learning disability, MTSS ensures that instructional gaps are ruled out before confirming a diagnosis. This protects students from being mislabeled due to poor teaching and ensures that those with true learning disabilities are identified (McIntosh & Goodman, 2016).

Misunderstanding 5: Time in a resource room is Tier 2 or Tier 3 intervention.

Reality: Resource rooms are a location, not a strategy—and grouping students by labels rather than needs undermines the purpose of intervention.

One of the most prevalent disconnects we see between MTSS research and practice is the assumption that if a student goes to a resource room, they are receiving intervention. Resource rooms are only physical spaces. Intervention can happen in a small group or individually in a space away from the large group, and intervention can happen within a general education classroom. But what happens in resource rooms is all too often not intervention at all. Sometimes, intervention simply isn't possible because of the way students are assigned to these spaces.

The problem is that resource rooms are typically filled any given class period with students whose commonality is that they all have IEPs—not with students who share the same skill needs. The placement is driven by paperwork, not data. Students with IEPs, however, have jagged profiles like every other student. Some may need support with reading fluency, while others need help with social regulation, written expression, or problem-solving in math. When students with dissimilar needs are grouped together for general "support," the special education teacher ends up playing a proverbial game of whack-a-mole, bouncing around from one student to the next, helping them complete classroom assignments and homework. But homework and assignment help are not interventions. In this grouping model, there is no room for targeted, evidence-based intervention. This general assistance doesn't systematically address any skill gaps, isn't a part of any of the MTSS tiers, and is a waste of intervention time.

True intervention systematically moves a student toward mastery of a specific skill using a proven, evidence-based practice. To do this, students must be grouped by shared needs, regardless of whether they have an IEP. For example, a group of students struggling with reading comprehension might participate in a structured intervention like reciprocal teaching, where they are explicitly taught how to summarize, question, clarify, and predict while reading. Some of the students in the group have IEPs, and others do not. This kind of grouping allows educators to focus on a specific skill using targeted, evidence-based strategies that meet the needs of all students in the group.

Misunderstanding 6: Students are pulled from core instruction to receive intervention.

Reality: When students need intervention, they receive both core instruction with their class and intervention delivered individually or in a small group.

A critical feature of MTSS is that students aren't removed from core instruction to receive intervention. What's happening in resource rooms that function as "catch-all" spaces for students with IEPs is not intervention and can even hinder learning if students are being pulled from core instruction to be there. When students are pulled out of core instruction for resource time, they miss critical learning opportunities.

Removing students from their core reading instruction to provide reading intervention, for example, is simply tracking, and, as we have noted, research shows tracking is ineffective. Instead, it's essential that core instruction is designed to be accessible for all students, with additional interventions added as a layer when needed.

In an integrated MTSS model, interventions are provided when core instruction isn't taking place—this applies to any subject, not just the traditional "core" areas like math or reading. This means that intervention can happen during independent work or small-group time, as long as no new instruction is being delivered. Although coordinating this can be straightforward in early childhood, when students spend most of the day with one teacher, it becomes much more complex in upper grades, when students are constantly moving between classes.

Nine Essential Components of the MTSS Framework

MTSS is built on three tiers of support, each addressing three critical areas: instruction, data, and collaborative planning (see Table 4.1).

TABLE 4.1 The Nine Essential Components of the MTSS Framework

TIER	INSTRUCTION	DATA	COLLABORATIVE PLANNING
Tier 1: Universal Supports	Core Instruction	Universal Screening	Core Review
Tier 2: Targeted Supports	Standardized Targeted Interventions	Progress Monitoring	Intervention Placement and Review
Tier 3: Intensive Supports	Customized or Intensive Interventions	Progress Monitoring and Diagnostics	Individual Problem-Solving

These components ensure that MTSS functions as a cohesive system in which every student receives the right support at the right time (Oregon Response to Instruction and Intervention, 2024). The same general structure can be applied to academic, behavioral, and social development. Let's explore these nine components and how they work together to form a proactive and effective MTSS framework.

Tier 1: Universal Supports

Tier 1 includes the practices we use with all students in the school. It is the foundation of the MTSS framework and sets the stage for success across all other tiers. At Tier 1, the focus is on ensuring that every student in every classroom has access to high-quality, evidence-based instruction that meets their diverse needs. Tier 1 is the most important part of the MTSS framework because this is where the opportunities for prevention are found.

1. **Instruction: Core Instruction**

   Excellent core instruction is the foundation of Tier 1—a proactive and inclusive approach that helps students thrive. Core instruction is built on practices proven by research, with the Visible Learning database serving as a key resource for these evidence-based strategies. Effective core instruction is intentionally designed to meet the diverse needs of all learners through UDL and differentiation, ensuring every student can engage meaningfully and learn. When core instruction is strong, most learning gaps are prevented without ever needing intervention.

2. **Data: Universal Screening**

   The universal screening of foundational skills is a critical component of Tier 1 and is typically conducted three times a year with *all* students. In comprehensive systems, schools screen foundational academic skills, such as phonemic awareness, phonics, and oral reading fluency in literacy or number sense and basic computation in math, as well as behavioral and social-emotional indicators like self-regulation and engagement. These targeted assessments help identify students who may need additional support and allow teachers to adjust their instruction proactively, addressing gaps before they widen. Universal screening ensures that Tier 1 instruction is effective for as many students as possible, fulfilling its role as the foundation of MTSS.

3. **Collaborative Planning: Core Review**

   At Tier 1, teams of educators regularly come together to review classroom-level data and assess the effectiveness of core instruction. These core review meetings ensure that decisions are grounded in evidence and focused on improving outcomes for all students. Core review meetings help teams answer essential questions: Are at least 80–90 percent of students meeting grade-level expectations? Are there patterns in the data indicating gaps in instruction, curriculum, or resources? If the data show that fewer than 80 percent of students are progressing as expected, the team works collaboratively to identify areas for improvement and make targeted adjustments to instruction.

Tier 2: Targeted Supports

Tier 2 provides targeted, small-group interventions for students who need more support than Tier 1 offers but do not require the intensity of Tier 3. These interventions enhance, rather than replace, core instruction and focus on addressing specific skill gaps or behavioral needs.

With structured, evidence-based practices, frequent progress monitoring, and collaborative planning, Tier 2 helps close gaps efficiently so students can return to success in the general classroom. This layer acts as a vital safety net, providing focused help to prevent the need for more intensive interventions.

1. **Instruction: Standardized Targeted Interventions**

   Students in Tier 2 receive small-group interventions *in addition to core instruction*. Intervention is focused on skill-based needs identified through data. The interventions are not teacher developed—they are programs and practices that are backed by research. As such, they need to be delivered with fidelity, consistent with the design that has been studied and proven effective. Tier 2 interventions are delivered in small groups, allowing for more individualized support and opportunities for feedback. The goal is to close gaps and exit intervention as soon as this happens.

2. **Data: Progress Monitoring**

   Progress monitoring is the foundation of decision-making at Tier 2. Teachers collect data every one to two weeks to measure how well students are responding to their interventions. These data points help track whether students are making progress toward specific goals and allow educators to make timely adjustments. Frequent progress monitoring keeps the focus on measurable growth and ensures that interventions remain aligned with student needs and that students get the intervention they need, as intensely as they need it, for as long as they need it, and no longer.

3. **Collaborative Planning: Intervention Placement and Review**

   Collaborative planning meetings keep Tier 2 interventions dynamic and responsive to student progress. Every six to eight weeks, teams of educators meet to analyze progress monitoring data and make informed decisions about each student's support plan. These meetings focus on ensuring that interventions are working and that students receive the appropriate level of support. During these reviews, teams assess whether students are meeting their intervention goals, which students are ready to exit Tier 2, and which students may require continued support or even more intensive interventions at Tier 3. Discussions include an analysis of progress trends, the fidelity of intervention implementation, and other factors that may impact student growth, such as attendance or external barriers. The team sets specific action steps, which may include adjustments to intervention groups, intensity levels, or instructional focus.

Tier 3: Intensive Supports

Tier 3 is designed for students with the most significant academic or behavioral needs, and those with inadequate progress with Tier 1 and Tier 2 supports. This tier provides the most individualized and intensive interventions within the MTSS framework. Only a small percentage of students typically require Tier 3.

1. **Instruction: Customized or Intensive Interventions**

   Tier 3 interventions are the highest level of intensity and dosage, often daily for thirty to forty-five minutes. These interventions target foundational skills or complex behavioral needs. Like Tier 2 interventions, Tier 3 interventions are *in addition to core instruction*, not a replacement for it. Tier 3 instruction is often one-on-one, but it can also occur in very small groups of two to three students if they share similar needs. These sessions are not tutoring or extra help with classwork; they are highly structured and use research-based practices and programs to address the root causes of a student's needs. Tier 3 requires a deep understanding of each student's needs and precise alignment with proven practices. The goal is to close gaps and enable students to access and benefit from core instruction alongside their peers.

2. **Data: Progress Monitoring and Diagnostics**

   The intensity of Tier 3 requires weekly progress monitoring and periodic diagnostic evaluations to provide detailed, actionable insights. Although frequent monitoring tracks how well students are responding to interventions, diagnostic assessments dig deeper to identify the root causes of a student's challenges. A diagnostic assessment could reveal an underlying need that requires a different or additional instructional approach. Regular data collection at this level allows teams to make precise adjustments to interventions. This combination ensures interventions remain highly targeted and responsive to each student's individual progress.

3. **Collaborative Planning: Individual Problem-Solving**

   Collaboration at Tier 3 is focused on developing and refining individualized support plans, formal or informal, for students with the most significant needs. Teams come together to analyze diagnostic data, review progress monitoring trends, and set specific goals tailored to the student's challenges. These meetings often include a wide range of stakeholders, such as general educators, special educators, interventionists, behavior specialists, school psychologists, and family members. The collaborative process is ongoing, with regular check-ins to evaluate progress, change strategies, and adjust intensity to maintain alignment with the student's evolving needs. By combining detailed problem-solving and consistent collaboration, Tier 3 ensures that even the most complex challenges are met with a structured, thoughtful approach.

Source: Adapted from Oregon Response to Instruction and Intervention (2024).

From the Classroom

Jefferson Elementary's MTSS in Action

At Jefferson Elementary, the Professional Learning Community (PLC) came together for their monthly meeting. Their session focused on improving reading outcomes for all students, ensuring that Tier 1 instruction was effective and that Tier 2 and Tier 3 interventions were aligned and impactful.

Mrs. Carter, the first-grade teacher, started the meeting by discussing how explicit phonics instruction was embedded into her daily reading block. "Core instruction has been going well overall," she said. "But I've noticed that a handful of students are still struggling with segmenting and blending sounds." The team explored adding more opportunities for interactive, multisensory activities, such as Elkonin boxes and movement-based phonics games, to strengthen engagement and accessibility.

The team reviewed the results of the fall universal screening, which highlighted a range of needs. Most students demonstrated proficiency in foundational reading skills, but several were flagged as needing additional support in phonemic awareness and decoding. Mrs. Carter pointed out two students, Emily and Noah, who were slightly below the benchmark but showed the potential to catch up with targeted instruction (Tier 2). Another student, Ben, was significantly below grade-level expectations and flagged for intensive intervention (Tier 3).

Next, the team engaged in core review, analyzing whether core instruction was meeting the needs of at least 80–90 percent of students. "Our data shows that 75 percent of students are meeting benchmarks," Mr. Simmons, the reading interventionist, noted. "This means we need to tweak our Tier 1 instruction." The team brainstormed ways to make their phonics lessons more robust. "We could dedicate more time to modeling blending during whole-class instruction," Mrs. Carter suggested. Mr. Simmons added, "And let's ensure all teachers consistently use the same routines during phonics instruction."

(Continued)

(Continued)

Emily and Noah were identified as needing Tier 2 small-group interventions focused on phonemic awareness. Mr. Simmons suggested using a standardized, evidence-based intervention program, such as *Phonemic Awareness* by Heggerty (2017), delivered three times a week for thirty minutes. "These small-group sessions will focus on segmenting and blending sounds to give them a solid foundation," he explained.

To ensure the effectiveness of Tier 2 interventions, the team planned to conduct progress monitoring every two weeks. This would enable them to track Emily and Noah's growth and determine whether the intervention was closing the gap. "If we see consistent improvement, we'll know the intervention is working," Mrs. Carter said. "If not, we'll need to intensify support or adjust the approach."

The team scheduled a review in six weeks to evaluate the progress of students receiving Tier 2 interventions. "We'll decide whether Emily and Noah are ready to exit the intervention, need continued support, or require Tier 3," Mr. Simmons explained.

Ben, who was flagged for Tier 3, required a more intensive, individualized intervention. The team decided to use 95 Percent Group materials to provide daily, one-on-one instruction targeting phoneme-grapheme correspondence and blending (https://www.95percentgroup.com/). In addition to weekly progress monitoring, the team had incorporated diagnostic assessments to pinpoint Ben's specific challenges.

"The diagnostic data revealed that Ben struggles with vowel sounds, so we'll prioritize that in his intervention," Mrs. Carter said.

"Ben needs a laser-focused approach to close the gap," Mr. Simmons explained. "These sessions will be short but powerful, with frequent opportunities for him to respond and apply what he's learning."

The team engaged in problem-solving to ensure Ben's intervention was as effective as possible. They set clear goals, outlined a timeline for monitoring progress, and coordinated with Ben's parents to reinforce skills at home.

Through the lens of MTSS, the Jefferson Elementary team demonstrated the power of a cohesive, data-driven approach to reading instruction. By aligning core instruction, targeted interventions, and intensive supports, they ensured that every student received what they needed to grow as readers. The focus on phonics at Tier 1 created a strong foundation, while intentional collaboration and evidence-based practices at Tiers 2 and 3 addressed the needs of students who required additional help. This thoughtful implementation of MTSS created a system in which all students had the opportunity to thrive.

Summary

Integrated MTSS provides a robust framework for delivering the right support to students at the right time, ensuring that no learner slips through the cracks. Educators have the power to shape student success through their approach to instruction and support. MTSS isn't just a system of tiers and interventions; it's a belief in the potential of every student and the ability of effective teaching to make a difference. The framework is grounded in a clear conviction: With strong instruction, almost all gaps in learning can be prevented, and with targeted intervention, even the most challenging gaps can be closed. By focusing on prevention, educators create classrooms where students thrive with high-quality, universally designed instruction. Teaching rooted in research isn't reserved for intervention; it's the standard for all students from the very beginning. The heart of MTSS is prevention.

When additional support is needed, intervention becomes a precise tool for addressing specific needs. Intervention time isn't spent offering general help with assignments or homework but is spent targeting critical skills using proven strategies. The success of intervention hinges on the collective effort of teachers, specialists, and support staff working together to review data, adjust strategies, and tailor interventions to meet students' evolving needs. Through regular progress monitoring and data-driven adjustments, educators ensure that the trajectory of students' growth improves.

MTSS reshapes what it means to support students. Prevention calls for purposeful teaching that reaches all learners. Intervention demands focus and expertise to address challenges. And collaboration unites educators around the shared goal of helping students succeed. MTSS offers more than a framework; it provides a path for schools to create a culture in which instruction anticipates needs, intervention builds mastery, and every student is given the opportunity to grow.

Learning Check

I can describe the three tiers of MTSS, including their purposes and implementation.

STRONGLY DISAGREE	DISAGREE	NEUTRAL	AGREE	STRONGLY AGREE
1	2	3	4	5

I can dispel common misunderstandings about the MTSS framework.

STRONGLY DISAGREE	DISAGREE	NEUTRAL	AGREE	STRONGLY AGREE
1	2	3	4	5

I can connect my understanding of MTSS to the broader concepts of universal design, differentiation, and data-driven decision-making to create a cohesive and responsive instructional framework.

STRONGLY DISAGREE	DISAGREE	NEUTRAL	AGREE	STRONGLY AGREE
1	2	3	4	5

5 Assessment Has the Power to Promote Growth

Learning Intention

- I am learning about assessment practices that lead to higher levels of learning and self-efficacy.

Success Criteria

- I can define formative and summative evaluation in terms of their function.
- I can design learning progressions to use as rubrics on transferable skills.
- I can support students to assess themselves.
- I can use high-quality feedback, rather than grades, as the foundation of how I communicate progress with students.

In this book, we'll use the term *mastery assessment* because although it shares several elements with standards-based grading, our approach has key differences (Jung, 2024). Ultimately, we aim to give you strong reasons and practical ideas to reduce the emphasis on grading.

When we refer to mastery, we're talking about outlining distinct stages of learning and understanding exactly where a student is along their growth path. This concept, drawn from 1970s psychological research (Haring et al., 1978), remains just as relevant today. Our version of mastery assessment

- highlights growth over static outcomes,
- prioritizes cultivating expert learners over mere content specialists, and
- promotes minimizing grading wherever possible.

Growth as the Focus

In mastery assessment, the goal is for every student to experience as much growth as possible. Although it's often necessary to report how students measure up to a standard by the end of the school year, this shouldn't be the focal point of classroom assessments or instructional practices. When we fixate on a singular benchmark for all students, we risk ignoring the richness of diversity in their "jagged learning profiles."

Learning doesn't conclude uniformly for all students by the last day of the academic year. Nor should it. Growth doesn't follow a set timetable, and neither do people! Schools aren't factories, and students are far from "standardized." Continuously evaluating students against fixed standards like "beginning" or "approaching" can stifle the growth mindset and self-efficacy that students—especially those with the greatest needs—desperately need. We should adopt assessment strategies that encourage remarkable growth and inspire students to reach beyond their limits. Shifting to this growth-oriented view means rethinking our assessment practices to better align with this vision.

Learning to Learn Takes Priority

As discussed earlier, some of the most impactful skills extend well beyond content knowledge and involve teaching students how to learn. This includes helping them set personal learning goals, monitor their progress, and persevere in achieving them (Efklides, 2011). These skills, which are transferable across many areas—such as communication, critical thinking, problem-solving, and collaboration—are essential.

Self-directed learners tend to be motivated, self-confident, aware of their abilities, curious, goal-focused, and proactive in their academic success (Roebers, 2017, p. 34; Zimmerman, 1989). However, these skills are neither formally taught nor assessed in many schools. Some report cards may include a section on "learning behaviors," but assessing these skills often lacks depth.

Our assessments should go beyond the narrow focus on academic standards and embrace these critical life skills, not as an afterthought, but as a core part of student growth. These transferable skills are, in many ways, just as important—if not more so—than content mastery. Because growth remains the priority, mastery assessment diverges from traditional standards-based grading.

Less Grading, More Learning

Mastery assessment revolves around understanding where students are in their learning journey, engaging in meaningful conversations with them about their progress, and celebrating growth, all while reducing the focus on scores and grades. Although grading is a common requirement, it often plays a minimal role in shaping effective teaching and learning. High-quality assessment can provide valuable insights when centered on growth, but when this information is reduced to a simple letter or number, it can undermine the very purpose of assessment—to improve learning and instruction.

The emotional and even physical harm caused by overreliance on grades is very real. Focusing on grading practices before addressing the bigger picture of assessment is like putting the cart before the horse. Although it's important to improve grading, it's just as essential to grade less—a lot less.

Misunderstandings of Formative and Summative

A true growth-focused learning environment is the opposite of one where students are stressed over grades, fixated on their GPAs, or constantly asking if something "counts" before deciding whether it's worth their effort. In a school that adopts mastery assessment, students aren't chasing the highest grade or hoping others fall behind—because grades are simply not part of the daily learning process or discussions.

One of the major misconceptions we've fallen into is thinking that "formative" and "summative" describe different kinds of assessments. We've been taught that a quick check-up on progress is formative while the final exam is summative—the final gets a grade but the check-up does not. But in reality, these terms don't describe the type of assessment, they refer to how we use the information from tests. Michael Scriven introduced these terms in 1967, and he created the term *formative and summative evaluation*—that these are the judgments during or at the end of an evaluation (Clinton & Hattie, 2024). Unfortunately, that definition has been muddled over time.

The biggest misunderstanding is thinking that "formative" and "summative" relate to how formal an assessment is. Picture this: you're at a professional development session, and the presenter asks the group, "If I assess students by walking around, observing their work, and casually asking them questions, is that formative or summative?" Before they can even finish, someone confidently jumps in, "Formative!" Heads nod in agreement. But they're actually wrong.

Now, this informal assessment could absolutely be used in a formative way—and often should be. But it could also be used summatively. The problem with labeling assessments as strictly formative or summative is that it implies that informal assessments aren't as valuable. It is less the test but rather the implications and interpretations of assessment occasions that are critical. We'll dive deeper into this later, but the key takeaway here is that even something as simple as a casual observation or a brief conversation can be used summatively if the purpose is to provide a final snapshot of learning. What makes an assessment summative is not the task itself but the permanence of the result. A grade becomes summative when it's recorded permanently—when it ends up on a report card or transcript. Just assigning a grade doesn't make it summative; it becomes summative when it's used to form a permanent record of the student's achievement. For instance, whenever an individual assignment grade is factored into a final course grade, it's being used summatively. Back when grades were written in ink on paper cards, final marks were unchangeable. Today, grades can and should evolve to reflect a student's current level of understanding at any given time.

On the flip side, a big, formal assessment—whether it's a project, paper, test, or performance—can also be used formatively (i.e., assist in improving learning, now). In fact, these large-scale assessments can frequently be used in a formative way—to guide future instruction rather than locking students into a permanent grade. How formal an assessment is has nothing to do with whether it should be formative or summative (Popham, 2006). Just because a task is formal doesn't mean it has to result in a grade or that the grade has to go in the grade book. Even if we do assign a grade, it doesn't have to be considered final or summative. The timing of the assessment—whether we're using it to inform instruction or summarize learning—determines whether it's formative or summative. We need ongoing assessment to inform our teaching day to day, and occasionally, we pause to take a snapshot of where students are. These snapshots don't require any special or more formal assessment; they are moments where we gather all the data to summarize the student's current learning status.

Talking About Assessment in a Growth-Centered Culture

So, how should we talk about assessment in a classroom that prioritizes growth? For starters, students don't need to know the terms "formative" and "summative." That doesn't mean we need to invent new jargon for these concepts, either. These words aren't secrets; they're just irrelevant to students if almost everything we do is formative, if nothing is set in stone until the very end, and if growth is the true goal. What matters is that students understand their efforts are being assessed continuously, with the goal of helping them grow, not just handing them a grade.

We should make it clear to our students that we're looking at all their efforts—from formal projects to everyday classroom interactions—to get a full picture of their progress. In this way, everything counts. Or, perhaps we don't need to talk about "assessment" at all. Maybe there's no real need to separate learning from assessment. Yes, we know that formative assessment is assessment for learning, and it's what has the potential to accelerate learning (formative evaluation $d = 0.55$; Corwin, 2024). When baking a cake, you can't tell where the flour ends and the sugar begins once it's all mixed together. Learning and formative assessment should be just as inseparable.

Questioning plays a pivotal role in this seamless blend of instruction and assessment. It is a powerful tool in a teacher's arsenal (questioning

$d = .68$; Corwin, 2024). Questioning isn't only about asking for answers; it's about using inquiry to assess understanding, guide instruction, and spark deeper thinking in real time. When done effectively, questioning serves as an ongoing, informal assessment that happens naturally during classroom interactions. This allows teachers to check for comprehension, uncover misconceptions, and adjust their teaching on the fly, without the need for separate, formal assessment periods. In this way, the boundaries between teaching and assessing dissolve. When done right, assessment is teaching. And assessment is learning.

Multiple Means of Expression

To create valid assessments, it's necessary to separate what we're measuring from how we measure it. Simply put, validity in assessment is the degree to which you actually measure what you intend to measure. Of course, we all aim for assessments reflecting the skills and knowledge we teach. After all, what's the point of assessing if it doesn't align with what's been taught? And yet, in schools across the board, assessments often fall short of this standard of validity.

When the assessment method interferes with what we're trying to measure, we've created what's known as a "threat to validity." In simple terms, the way we tested compromised the accuracy of the results. For example, a timed test can easily become more about who handles time pressure better than who has mastered the content. If the assessment approach doesn't match particular students' needs, we can make faulty decisions about their learning or progress.

Validity issues arise when students are only given one way to demonstrate their knowledge. This creates an unfair advantage for students who excel in that specific method of expression, not because they've grasped the content better, but because they're simply more comfortable with that format. The result? The method, not the understanding, becomes the differentiator.

As an example, some students might thrive when delivering presentations but feel completely lost when it comes to written exams. Others may easily sail through a test, only to freeze up when asked to speak in front of a group. Then there are those who excel at creating visual projects but struggle when put on a timer. And let's be honest: Many of us would find sitting down for a timed, multiple-choice test (even on a topic we know inside and out) nerve-wracking. Some of us are "over-analyzers," capable of convincing ourselves that every option could be the correct answer.

Think back to your own experiences. Maybe you recall a moment during a key exam—a licensing test or certification—where you were sure you knew the material but didn't do as well as expected. The frustration sticks with you, not because you lacked the knowledge, but because the test format tripped you up. If that memory still stings a bit, it's time to shake it off. The issue wasn't you—it was the test design. The way you were assessed didn't allow you to showcase what you really knew. (Take that, exam board!)

Until we actively identify and remove these threats to validity, our assessments will continue to be plagued by inequities—and the solution lies in providing students with choices.

Choice: The Path to Fairness

As we discovered earlier in reflecting on our own teaching preferences, no single method of performance works as a valid assessment for everyone. And, equally, there's no one method that presents a challenge to validity for everyone. What works for one student might be a stumbling block for another. This variability in how students perform under certain conditions influences our ability to see their true understanding if we limit assessment to a single method. For example, if a timed test is the only option, students with test anxiety or those who need extra time may be unfairly penalized—not because they didn't learn the material, but because the method didn't suit their needs.

In other words, the test's validity is compromised when we fail to offer alternative ways to demonstrate learning. Ironically, our attempts to "level the playing field" by giving everyone the same tests actually create inequities. This is where the idea that "fair is not always equal" really comes into play. Just think of how much more students could show us if we allowed them to choose how to demonstrate their knowledge and removed barriers like time limits. Giving students options doesn't just promote fairness—it boosts their engagement and motivation (CAST, 2024). After all, when students have a say in how they express their learning, they're far more invested in the process.

That said, offering choice isn't about lowering expectations or giving students an easier route. The level of proficiency required doesn't change—only the method of showing it does. Suppose the goal is to assess a student's ability to build and defend an argument with evidence. In that case, the standard remains the same, whether that argument is presented in a speech, a video, a paper, or an oral conference with a teacher. We're simply allowing students to show their understanding in the way that best suits their strengths. Sometimes, it can be as simple as giving them the option to present while standing in front of the class or seated at their desk.

Ultimately, the only way to remove validity threats from our assessments is to offer students choices in how they show what they've learned. There are countless ways to assess the same skill or understanding, but if we want those assessments to be truly valid, we need to eliminate the barriers standing in the way. But how do we decide which choices to offer? This requires careful thought about which options will break down barriers for all students and accurately reflect their learning.

We need to anticipate barriers based on data, prior performance, and information from everyday interactions. By carefully analyzing patterns in student performance, we can identify specific threats to validity that may impact particular groups or individuals. For example, suppose we notice that students with strong conceptual understanding consistently underperform on timed tests, or that those who excel in written responses struggle in oral presentations. In that case, these patterns highlight a potential mismatch between the method of assessment and what we're trying to measure. Understanding these patterns allows us to offer the right choices that address the most common barriers without lowering expectations. The goal is not to provide an endless array of options but to thoughtfully design assessments that remove obstacles while still accurately measuring the targeted skills and knowledge. By offering alternatives that align with students' strengths, we can ensure that the method of assessment doesn't become a barrier to demonstrating mastery.

What presents a barrier today might disappear tomorrow. Because threats to validity can shift over time, there will be instances when we didn't foresee a specific need or barrier, affecting the assessment. When this happens, it's our responsibility to recognize that the results may not accurately reflect students' true abilities, and we must discount any assessment that isn't a valid measure of their learning. Often, we already have enough evidence from other interactions or previous assessments—paired with a conversation with the student—to make an informed judgment without creating a new assessment. Sometimes, an upcoming assessment will naturally cover the same skills or understanding. In these cases, we don't always need to offer a "make-up" opportunity; the information we need may already be available from other sources.

From the Classroom

Firm Goals, Flexible Means

Ms. Ramirez had a hunch something wasn't quite right. Jayden, her most vocal and engaged student, had absolutely bombed the latest math test. It didn't make sense—he was always the first to raise his hand, easily explaining concepts to classmates during group work. Meanwhile, Emily, who tended to sit quietly in the back and dreaded group discussions, had aced it. Ms. Ramirez knew she needed to dig deeper.

At lunch, she pulled Jayden aside. "Jayden, I know you get this. I've seen you help others in class, but your test says otherwise. What happened?" Jayden sighed. "It's the timer," he said, rubbing his temples. "I get so stressed about finishing in time that my brain just . . . stops working."

That evening, Ms. Ramirez replayed the day in her mind. She remembered how Emily thrived when working independently, flying through written work when left alone but completely freezing during class presentations. Meanwhile, Jayden had no problem talking through problems but seemed to crumble under the pressure of a written, timed test.

The next day, Ms. Ramirez stood at the front of the class with a new plan. "Alright, everyone," she began. "For our next assessment, you'll have two options: You can take a written test like usual, or you can

(Continued)

(Continued)

complete a creative project where you apply the same math concepts to solve a real-world problem. Choose the one that lets you show your best work."

When the assessments came back, Jayden enthusiastically tackled the project option, creating an elaborate mock budget for a summer carnival, calculating costs, ticket prices, and even profits. It was clear he had mastered the material, and the pressure of the clock was nowhere in sight. On the other hand, Emily stuck with the written test and nailed it again, as expected.

By offering options aligned with each student's strengths, Ms. Ramirez removed the barriers that prevented them from fully showing what they knew. The results were clear: when students were given the right tools, the true depth of their understanding could finally shine through.

Conversation as Assessment

Conversation isn't just a platform for discussing informal assessment; it is an informal assessment, and often the most effective form of assessment is a simple conversation. Through meaningful dialogue, teachers can gather rich insights into students' understanding, struggles, and thought processes in ways that traditional assessments often miss. But conversation doesn't stop at gathering data—it's also a powerful tool for fostering a positive and supportive learning environment. When students engage in a genuine conversation with their teacher, they feel heard, valued, and encouraged, which fuels motivation and deepens their connection to learning. In contrast, formal assessments can sometimes create anxiety or distance, undermining the very engagement we strive to cultivate.

Using student-teacher conferences as a form of assessment profoundly impacts learning (Hattie & Timperley, 2007). These one-on-one discussions offer a unique chance to give elaborated feedback in a way that standard assessments rarely can. In a conference, a teacher can address specific strengths and areas for growth tailored to that individual student's needs. Rather than the generic, one-size-fits-all feedback that often accompanies graded assessments, conferencing allows for targeted, actionable guidance that students can immediately apply to their work. This personalized feedback goes beyond just correcting mistakes—it directs students toward improvement in clear, specific ways directly relevant to their own learning journey.

Conferences offer the potential to build strong, trust-based relationships between students and teachers. Student-teacher relationships matter to students' outcomes ($d = 0.72$; Corwin, 2024). When students know they have a safe space to talk openly about their progress, they are more likely to engage honestly with their learning and take ownership of their growth. These interactions transform assessment into a partnership in which both teacher and student work together to identify next steps and celebrate achievements, creating an environment in which students feel supported in every aspect of their development (Pianta, 1999).

Learning Progressions as Rubrics

The pressure to assign grades often leads to rubrics that focus heavily on points and rigid procedures. This process can be time-consuming on its own, but when combined with the task of giving students multiple ways to demonstrate learning, it might seem overwhelming. But there's good news: We can create measures that are versatile to be used across all of the options for expression we give students. This approach requires moving away from traditional rubrics toward rubrics centered on growth (Jung, 2024). The two main issues that need addressing are (1) the tendency to conflate skills with tasks and (2) the focus on what's missing rather than what's being learned.

You might be wondering how rubrics can work when students have different options for showing what they've learned. Fortunately, focusing on skills rather than tasks makes this process much simpler. Instead of creating a separate rubric for each type of project, we use learning progressions as "task-independent" rubrics. These progressions focus on the specific skill or understanding you want to assess, regardless of how the student chooses to demonstrate it.

For example, if the skill we're assessing is summarizing, we don't need separate rubrics for each text. We don't even need separate rubrics for different formats of content, like a book, an article, and a presentation. We can create one progression that can be used to assess summarizing, and it applies across all formats (see Table 5.1). The rubric measures the student's ability to summarize, not how well they've used a specific medium. This method keeps the focus on learning and makes the assessment process more efficient, fair, and *valid*.

TABLE 5.1 Rubric for Assessing Summarizing Skill

DISCOVERING KEY IDEAS	MAKING CONNECTIONS	SUMMARIZING WITH PURPOSE	SUMMARIZING WITH INSIGHT
I can identify important parts of the content and point out ideas that stand out to me. I notice interesting connections between ideas and share what sparks my curiosity about how the content is organized.	**I can** highlight the main ideas in the content and select details that are connected to these ideas. I confidently explain in my own words my understanding of what the content is about in a way that is clear and thoughtful.	**I can** summarize the content, showing how the purpose, main ideas, and key details fit together. I organize my thoughts logically, express them clearly, and explain the content in a way that helps others understand its meaning.	**I can** create a clear and focused summary that reflects the content creator's purpose and integrates the most essential details. I weave ideas together, demonstrate deep understanding, and express the content in my own thoughtful and original way.

When we rethink assessment and focus on clear learning progressions for each skill or understanding, we can create rubrics that grow alongside our students over the course of the year. These rubrics also have the flexibility to meet each student where they are in their learning journey. In some cases, we may need to add levels to either end of the rubric to capture where a particular student is in their progression. A one-size-fits-all rubric doesn't cut it. Our rubrics should be flexible enough to adapt at any point, accurately reflecting where each student stands and where they need to go next. Traditional rubrics that focus on what's wrong can't do this. There's only so much you can take away before you're left with a "barely trying" category. But with a learning progression, there's always a next step. By using rubrics that are directly linked to the core skills we value, we can expand or adjust them as needed while keeping the focus on the same key learning goals for all students—*firm goals, flexible pathways, and variable paces.*

Assess With Students

As educators, we have a choice in how we approach assessment. We can take on the role of the critic, pointing out what's missing or flawed, or we can act as mentors, helping students reflect on their progress and identify the next steps. A critic's job is highlighting errors and assigning grades based on what was wrong. This position holds the power and authority, leaving students feeling evaluated rather than supported.

Being a mentor, however, transforms the assessment process into a collaborative effort. As mentors, we sit beside our students, guiding them as they set their own goals, identify areas for improvement, and develop strategies for growth. We don't need to be the "Simon Cowell" of the classroom, constantly critiquing; instead, we can be like the vocal coach who works behind the scenes, encouraging students and giving them actionable feedback to help them improve. Our role is to help them reach their potential, not to judge them.

Mentors assess with students, using feedback as a tool to uncover the next steps in learning. It's not just about assessing content knowledge; we're also helping students develop social and emotional skills like communication, empathy, and problem-solving (Jones & Bouffard, 2012). Focusing on these skills not only benefits students' personal development but also enhances their academic performance (Durlak et al., 2011).

As mentors, we empower students to take ownership of their learning, developing the metacognitive skills they need to become lifelong learners. When students see us as partners in their learning process, they're more likely to seek help, take risks, and engage in deeper reflection (Zachary & Fain, 2022). This shift in mindset allows students to take a more active role in assessment, setting them on the path to becoming self-directed learners.

Mentorship also provides the ideal context for teaching critical thinking and self-assessment skills. By encouraging students to reflect on their work, evaluate their strengths and weaknesses, and consider what learning strategies they want to try next, we help them build the metacognitive skills essential for long-term success (Dweck, 2006). This focus on reflection and self-efficacy nurtures independent thinkers equipped to take control of their learning journeys.

Constructive feedback, focused on helping students grow rather than just pointing out errors, is essential for any learner. When feedback is directly aligned with learning goals but personalized to fit where a student currently is in their journey, it can be incredibly effective ($d = .50$; Corwin, 2024; see also Black & Wiliam, 1998b; Nicol & Macfarlane-Dick, 2006; Wiliam, 2011). This kind of feedback helps students see their own potential for improvement, boosting their motivation and engagement.

Research consistently highlights key qualities of effective feedback. A helpful way to remember these qualities is the acronym PEACE (Jung, 2024).

- **Prompt**. Students need feedback soon after completing an assignment while they're still thinking about the material. Prompt feedback ensures that students can reflect on what they've just learned and apply those insights to future tasks. If feedback is delayed, students may lose touch with the material, making it harder to integrate the guidance they receive (Shute, 2008).
- **Encouraging**. Feedback should highlight a student's strengths while providing constructive suggestions for improvement. Instead of focusing on what went wrong, we should guide students toward what they can do next. This positive framing can build confidence and a growth mindset, which we know leads to more resilient, motivated learners (Dweck, 2006; Shute, 2008).
- **Always**. Feedback is most effective when it's an ongoing conversation rather than a one-time event. Regular, continuous feedback throughout the learning process helps students make adjustments as they go, keeping them engaged and motivated. It promotes a continuous improvement culture, where students constantly refine their understanding (Black & Wiliam, 1998a; Nicol & Macfarlane-Dick, 2006).
- **Connected**. Feedback should be specific and tied directly to learning objectives. General praise or vague critique doesn't

help students know what to focus on. Connecting feedback to clear learning goals ensures students understand exactly where they're doing well and where they need to improve (Black & Wiliam, 1998b).

- **Engaging**. Effective feedback involves students in the process. Encouraging self-assessment and peer feedback gives students a sense of ownership over their learning. By reflecting on their work and that of their peers, students develop important metacognitive skills, making them more independent learners in the long run (Black & Wiliam, 1998a; Nicol & Macfarlane-Dick, 2006).

In addition, teachers can integrate the evidence around wise feedback to invite students to use the feedback provided. As Cohen et al. (1999) and Yeager et al. (2014) note, students—especially those at risk of academic underperformance or failure—may instead misinterpret critical instructional feedback as a sign that the teacher lacks confidence in and is negatively biased toward the learner. The goal of wise feedback is to "assuage mistrust by emphasizing the teacher's high standards and belief that the student was capable of meeting those standards" (Yeager et al., 2014, p. 804). The intervention is relatively simply: The teacher makes an express comment that clearly communicates to the student that they have high expectations *and* the belief that the student can reach those expectations. Thus, the feedback is designed to help students reach the expectations that the teacher knows they can attain. Educator Breana Bayraktar (2021) provides the following examples of wise feedback:

Step 1: Communicate high expectations.

- "I know it feels like this is a very challenging task I'm asking you to do—and it is."
- "Learning how to write a lab report is a new skill that you haven't been asked to do before, but it will help you to think about your skill set as a scientist does when you write your research proposal."
- "Giving a presentation in front of the whole class can feel scary, but it's really good practice for job interviews."

Step 2: Explain that you believe the student can meet the expectations.

- "Your work to this point demonstrates that you already can do __________ and __________ well."
- "You earned a score of __________ on the last quiz, which shows me that you understand the foundational concepts for the project."
- "Your first draft had some really excellent points, so I know that you are capable of meeting the expectations for the final essay."

Step 3: Provide actionable feedback that demonstrates support.

- "The feedback I gave you on your draft is where you should start as you write the next version. I look forward to reading your final paper!"
- "Looking at your quiz responses, you should start with a review of __________ and __________ concepts so that you feel as comfortable with them as you do with __________, which you did really well on."

From the Classroom

PEACE Feedback That Fuels Learning

In Mr. Davis's eighth-grade science class, students were tasked with designing their own experiments to test different hypotheses about plant growth. The assignment was part of a broader unit on ecosystems, and students were excited to take on the role of scientists.

Lila, who was usually quiet but highly observant, was investigating the effect of different light sources on plant growth. She meticulously set up her experiment but struggled with articulating her hypothesis clearly. Mr. Davis provided **prompt** feedback during her planning phase. "Lila, you've got a solid experiment here, but your hypothesis could be clearer. How about we focus on the specific variables you're testing—what will you expect to see with the different light sources?"

Lila nodded, taking the suggestion in stride. Mr. Davis then provided **encouraging** feedback. "You've done a great job identifying the types of light you'll use—that shows you're thinking critically. Now, let's work on refining how you explain what you expect to happen."

Throughout the week, Mr. Davis consistently checked in with his students. His feedback wasn't reserved for the final project—it was **always** part of the process, guiding them as they adjusted their methods and refined their hypotheses. He ensured that the feedback was **connected** to the learning objectives. As Lila revised her hypothesis, he made sure she understood how this step aligned with the larger goal of mastering experimental design.

Later in the week, students shared their experimental plans with peers for review. Lila paired up with Marcus, a fellow student studying soil types' impact on plant growth. During the **engaging** peer review session, Marcus pointed out that Lila's data collection plan might need more detail. Lila reflected on his comments and made adjustments to her experiment, strengthening her approach.

Finally, the class used Google Docs to provide written feedback to one another on their experiment plans. Mr. Davis also encouraged students to self-assess their work using a checklist based on the project rubric. This peer review and self-assessment process allowed students like Lila to take ownership of their learning, actively engaging with feedback and refining their projects as they went.

As the week ended, the students not only strengthened their experiments but also developed a deeper understanding of the scientific process—and the power of constructive feedback in helping them grow.

Self-Assessment

Self-assessment gives students the ability to take control of their own learning. It involves more than having students grade themselves; it means becoming more self-aware, learning how to reflect on progress, and figuring out where to go next. When students assess their own work, they shift from being passive participants in the classroom to active learners who can recognize their strengths, identify areas for improvement, and make informed decisions about their learning. Self-assessment in the classroom builds critical thinking, problem-solving, and the ability to direct one's own learning. It allows students to take responsibility for their progress, building confidence and promoting a growth mindset. For self-assessment to work, though, it can't be a one-off task at the end of a unit. Instead, it should happen regularly, with students reflecting on their learning before, during, and after every significant lesson or project.

Phases of Self-Assessment

Self-assessment works best when broken down into three key phases: before, during, and after learning. Each phase allows students to reflect at different points in their learning journey.

Before Learning: Setting Intentions

Before jumping into a lesson or assignment, students should take a moment to reflect on their starting point. This phase is all about preparation—making sure students understand what's expected, how it relates to what they already know, and how they're going to approach it.

Helpful questions for students to ask themselves at this stage might include, "What is the objective of this lesson or task?", "How does this connect to my personal learning goals?", "What do I already know about this topic?", and "What's the best way for me to prepare?"

A student who is about to begin a project on ecosystems might ask herself, "What do I already know about food chains, and how can I apply that knowledge here?" By reflecting on prior knowledge, the student is setting themselves up to dive in with more focus and confidence.

During Learning: Staying on Track

Once the work begins, self-assessment becomes a way for students to stay engaged and make sure they're heading in the right direction. This phase is all about real-time reflection—thinking about what's working, what isn't, and adjusting strategies as needed.

During learning, students might ask themselves, "Am I meeting the goals for this lesson?", "What strategies are helping me stay focused and succeed?", and "What am I finding difficult or confusing, and how can I work through that?"

For example, a student like Jayden might hit a roadblock while working on a math assignment. By asking, "Why is this particular problem giving me trouble?" he can identify the issue and either seek help or switch up his approach to get back on track.

After Learning: Reflecting and Planning Ahead

Once a task is completed, self-assessment doesn't stop. Students need to reflect on their performance, reflect on what they did well, and think about how to improve next time. This phase is where the real growth happens—it's about celebrating successes and learning from challenges.

Examples of questions to ask after a task include, "What worked well in this task, and what didn't?", "How did I meet the learning objectives?", and "What can I do differently next time to improve?"

Imagine Marcus, who's just finished a history essay. He might reflect, "I think I nailed the argument, but I struggled with citing my sources correctly." This kind of reflection helps Marcus focus on a specific area for improvement, giving him a clear direction for the next assignment.

Implementing Self-Assessment

Here are a few ways to make self-assessment more effective and meaningful in the classroom:

1. Use mastery rubrics

   Mastery rubrics aren't only for teachers to use. Providing students with clear expectations through learning intentions, success criteria, and mastery rubrics gives focus and structure to self-assessment. This makes the self-assessment process clearer and more focused.

2. Introduce learning logs

   Keeping a learning journal or log helps students reflect regularly on what they've learned, what strategies worked, and what they need to improve. This can be an ongoing tool that encourages deeper thinking about their learning process.

3. Schedule peer feedback

   Sometimes students can learn just as much from their peers as they can from their teachers. Pairing students for peer feedback can give them a new perspective and help them see their work through a different lens.

4. Provide guided questions

   Offering students a set of reflection questions, like the ones in Table 5.2 below, helps guide them through the self-assessment process, especially if they're new to it. We aren't suggesting you use *all* of these questions on any given assignment, but select the ones you want students to focus on using.

TABLE 5.2 Reflection Questions

BEFORE LEARNING	DURING LEARNING	AFTER LEARNING
What is the objective of this lesson or task? How does it relate to my individual goals?	What questions are coming up for me during the class? Am I recording them in any way?	What was the purpose of today's class?
What is my prior knowledge about this topic?	How invested am I in this material? How confident do I feel in my learning? What steps could I take to boost my interest and confidence?	How does the material from today's class build upon what we've previously learned?
What would be the most effective way to prepare for this class?	Am I experiencing any difficulties with my motivation? If so, can I recall how this course ties into my objectives?	To what extent did I utilize available resources during class?
Where would be best for me to sit during class to optimize my learning experience? What should I be doing to stay focused?	In what ways is the teaching aiding my learning? How can I capitalize on these benefits?	To what extent did I meet the success criteria of the lesson?
What questions do I have about this topic that I want to explore further?	In what ways is the teaching hindering my learning? How can I compensate for these obstacles?	What steps can I take now to address my questions and confusion?
What resources do I need to acquire to learn this? How will I make sure I have access to them?	Which approaches am I utilizing that are proving effective or ineffective in assisting me with my learning?	What was the most interesting aspect of today's class for me?
What are all the steps I need to take to complete this task successfully?	To what degree am I utilizing all of the available resources to help me learn?	What strategies or methods worked well for me today that I can use again in the future?

BEFORE LEARNING	DURING LEARNING	AFTER LEARNING
How much time will I need to complete this task?	Which of my questions or misunderstandings have I cleared up? How did I manage to get them cleared up?	What new information or ideas in class conflict with my prior knowledge or understanding?
How can I improve my performance if I have done something similar before?	Which questions or misunderstandings remain, and what's my plan for resolving them?	What aspects of class today did not work well for me and need to be changed?
How long and how often do I plan to study for this course?	What additional resources might I need to complete this task? What steps should I take to obtain them?	What mistakes did I make, and what areas do I need to clarify?
Which areas of the course material should I prioritize based on my current level of understanding?	Can I distinguish between critical information and trivial details? If not, how will I go about making this distinction?	What will be the most memorable takeaway from this class in five years?
Why is it essential to learn this course material?	What is the most difficult or confusing aspect of this task for me?	If I were to teach this lesson, what changes would I make?
How will I track my progress and actively monitor my learning in this course?	What can I do differently to address these challenges and confusion during my learning process?	What advice would I offer to a friend about how to maximize their learning in this class?

Source: Jung (2024) and Tanner (2012).

Connecting Self-Assessment and Feedback

Self-assessment and feedback are important in their own right, but they are magical when combined. A truly impactful self-assessment needs to be embedded into a conversation between the student and the teacher. Teachers can guide students in reflecting more deeply and offering insights the students might have missed, creating a powerful tool for student growth.

For example, after a self-assessment, a teacher might review a student's reflections and comment, "You've recognized that your analysis is strong, but let's work on how you're structuring your arguments. Here are a few strategies you can try next time." This feedback reinforces the student's reflection while giving them concrete steps to improve.

From the Classroom

Improving Writing With Reflection, Self-Assessment, and Feedback

In Mrs. Clark's ninth-grade English class, her students were working on a literary analysis essay. Before starting, each student completed a self-assessment form reflecting on their writing strengths and weaknesses, particularly with constructing arguments and using evidence.

As they wrote, students paused to check their progress using a rubric, asking themselves questions like, "Is my thesis clear? Am I backing up my points with strong evidence?" This helped keep them on track throughout the process.

At the end of the project, students wrote a brief reflection in their learning journals, highlighting what went well and where they still needed to grow. Mrs. Clark reviewed these reflections, offering personalized feedback to each student. "You've identified that your argument is strong, but your transitions between paragraphs could be smoother. Let's work on that for the next draft."

For students like Leah, this process was eye-opening. She said, "I knew I was struggling with transitions, but hearing Mrs. Clark's feedback gave me a clear direction for how to fix it next time."

By teaching students to reflect on their learning at different stages, we're helping them become more independent, motivated, and resilient learners. When students regularly assess themselves, they start to see learning as an ongoing process of improvement rather than a series of grades. And when combined with thoughtful teacher feedback, self-assessment can unlock incredible academic and personal growth. It's all about empowering students to take charge of their learning, giving them the tools they need to succeed today—and long after they leave the classroom.

Summary

Adopting a growth-oriented approach to classroom assessment is transformative—not only for the way we evaluate student progress but also for how students perceive their own learning. By shifting the focus from grading to mastery and growth, we empower students to take ownership of their learning journey, promoting self-efficacy and resilience. This shift redefines assessment from a series of static checkpoints to an ongoing, dynamic conversation, in which the goal is continuous improvement rather than a final, unchangeable score.

The primary goal of mastery assessment is ensuring that every student experiences maximum growth. Although it's necessary to report how students measure up to standards by the end of the school year, focusing solely on benchmarks can ignore the richness of diverse learning profiles and jagged edges. Growth doesn't follow a set timetable, and neither do students. If we assess students solely against fixed standards like "beginning" or "approaching," we risk stifling the growth mindset that students need to thrive.

Some of the most valuable skills extend beyond content knowledge. These include setting personal learning goals, monitoring progress, and persevering (Efklides, 2011). Self-directed learners—those who are aware of their abilities, curious, and proactive—tend to be more successful. However, schools often fail to assess these skills formally. Mastery assessment puts learning behaviors and transferable skills, such as communication, critical thinking, and collaboration, at the center, rather than treating them as secondary considerations.

Ultimately, the tools and strategies presented here—task-independent rubrics, formative assessments, peer and self-assessment, and feedback as the primary mode of communication—are all designed to cultivate a classroom environment where learning is fluid, barriers are removed, and every student has the opportunity to thrive. As educators, our role is to mentor and guide students, offering them the challenge, support, flexibility, and feedback they need to catapult their growth as students and lifelong learners.

Learning Check

I can define formative and summative evaluation in terms of their function.

STRONGLY DISAGREE	DISAGREE	NEUTRAL	AGREE	STRONGLY AGREE
1	2	3	4	5

I can design learning progressions to use as rubrics on transferable skills.

STRONGLY DISAGREE	DISAGREE	NEUTRAL	AGREE	STRONGLY AGREE
1	2	3	4	5

I can support students to assess themselves.

STRONGLY DISAGREE	DISAGREE	NEUTRAL	AGREE	STRONGLY AGREE
1	2	3	4	5

I can use high-quality feedback, rather than grades, as the foundation of how I communicate progress with students.

STRONGLY DISAGREE	DISAGREE	NEUTRAL	AGREE	STRONGLY AGREE
1	2	3	4	5

Conclusion

At the heart of this book is a vision: a world where all learners, regardless of labels, abilities, or backgrounds, have access to impactful educational experiences. Achieving this vision requires more than using the "best of the best" teaching techniques. It demands a deeper shift in how we view variability among and within learners. Instead of addressing differences as challenges, inclusive educators embrace variation as the norm and design proactively. Effective practices are critical, but creating truly inclusive environments requires seeing each learner as unique, with a complex, "jagged" learning profile and boundless potential.

The mindframes outlined in this book are more than theories; they are actionable beliefs, thoughts, and attitudes that have the power to transform classrooms, schools, and communities. Grounded in more than thirty-five years of research through the Visible Learning database, these mindframes underscore a truth: How we think as educators fundamentally shapes the outcomes we achieve. The stories we tell ourselves about what's possible, who belongs, and who can succeed underscore our classroom realities. When we embrace mindframes that prioritize high expectations and collective responsibility, we're not only shifting practice but rewriting those stories.

Simply having learner variability within the same physical classroom walls is not inclusion. "Least restrictive environment" is a low bar. Inclusion requires us to tear down the invisible walls that keep students from experiencing the full benefits of instruction. These mindframes lead us to plan everything we do with variation in mind—supports are baked in proactively from the start, rather than added on as a reaction. We create instructional environments that work better for everyone by removing barriers for students who face the greatest challenges.

As you consider the five mindframes we've outlined, we ask you to contemplate the world you hope to create. We envision an inclusive society in which all people are respected and valued and know they can contribute to their communities. We want students, young and old, to develop a profound sense of belonging, knowing they are perfect the way they are. To this end, our students are counting on us to question the practices we have inherited, reflect on their impact, and engage in continuous improvement. This work demands relentless optimism, grounded in evidence, that we *can* create classrooms and schools where labels lose their power to limit, where every learner feels they belong, and where every educator sees themselves as a change agent. The question isn't whether this transformation can happen. Every child *can* receive the special education they deserve. The question is whether we are ready to make it happen. The evidence is clear. The tools are within reach.

References

American Psychological Association (APA). (2015). *Stress in America: Paying with our health*. https://www.apa.org/news/press/releases/stress/2014/stress-report.pdf

Bayraktar, B. (2021, February 2). Tip: Give "wise" feedback. *Tips for Teaching Professors*. https://higheredpraxis.substack.com/p/tip-give-wise-feedback

Berman, J., Graham, L., Bellert, A., & McKay-Brown, L. (2024). *Responsive teaching for sustainable learning: A framework for inclusive education*. Taylor & Francis.

Black, P., & Wiliam, D. (1998a). Assessment and classroom learning. *Assessment in Education: Principles, Policy & Practice, 5*(1), 7–74.

Black, P., & Wiliam, D. (1998b). Inside the black box: Raising standards through classroom assessment. *Phi Delta Kappan, 80*(2), 139–148.

Blannin, J., Wood, C., Stubbs, P., & Hattie, J. (2024). Informing professional learning interventions with evidence-based analysis of student feedback: Implications for software use and learning clarity. *Computers and Education Open, 7*, 100211.

Braddock, J. H. (1990). *Tracking: Implications for student race-ethnic subgroups* (Report No. 1). Office of Educational Research and Improvement.

Bryk, A., & Schneider, B. (2002). *Trust in schools: A core resource for improvement*. Russell Sage Foundation.

Capp, M. J. (2017). The effectiveness of universal design for learning: A meta-analysis of literature between 2013 and 2016. *International Journal of Inclusive Education, 21*(8), 791–807.

CAST. (2024). *About universal design for learning*. https://www.cast.org/resources/about-universal-design-for-learning/

Castejón, A., & Zancajo, A. (2015). Educational differentiation policies and the performance of disadvantaged students across OECD countries. *European Educational Research Journal, 14*(3–4), 222–239.

Chita-Tegmark, M., Gravel, J. W., Maria De Lourdes, B. S., Domings, Y., & Rose, D. H. (2011). Using the universal design for learning framework to support culturally diverse learners. *Journal of Education, 192*(1), 17–22.

Clinton, J., & Hattie, J. (2024). Revisiting and expanding Scriven's fallacies about formative and summative evaluation. *Journal of Multidisciplinary Evaluation, 20*(47), 13–23.

Cohen, G. L., Steele, C. M., & Ross, L. D. (1999). The mentor's dilemma: Providing critical feedback across the racial divide. *Personality and Social Psychology Bulletin, 25*(10), 1302–1318.

Cole, S. M., Murphy, H. R., Frisby, M. B., & Robinson, J. (2023). The relationship between special education placement and high school outcomes. *The Journal of Special Education, 57*(1), 13–23. https://doi.org/10.1177/00224669221097945

Corwin. (2024, November). Global research database (Version 1.3). *Visible Learning Meta*^{X}. https://www.visiblelearningmetax.com/

Costa, A., & Kallick, B. (2008). *Leading and learning with habits of mind: 16 characteristics for success*. ASCD.

Cuban, L. (2020). Reforming the grammar of schooling again and again. *American Journal of Education, 126*(4), 665–671.

Dack, H. (2019). Understanding teacher candidate misconceptions and concerns about differentiated instruction. *The Teacher Educator, 54*(1), 22–45.

Darling-Hammond, L. (2015). *The flat world and education: How America's commitment to equity will determine our future*. Teachers College Press.

Datnow, A., & Park, V. (2018). Opening or closing doors for students? Equity and data use in schools. *Journal of Educational Change, 19*, 131–152.

Domina, T., McEachin, A., Hanselman, P., Agarwal, P., Hwang, N., & Lewis, R. W. (2019). Beyond tracking and detracking: The dimensions of organizational differentiation in schools. *Sociology of Education, 92*(3), 293–322.

Donnellan, A. M. (1984). The criterion of the least dangerous assumption. *Behavioral Disorders, 9*(2), 141–150.

Dunn, D. S., & Burcaw, S. (2013). Disability identity: Exploring narrative accounts of disability. *Rehabilitation Psychology, 58*(2), 148–157. https://doi.org/10.1037/a0031691

Durlak, J. A., Weissberg, R. P., Dymnicki, A. B., Taylor, R. D., & Schellinger, K. B. (2011). The impact of enhancing students' social and emotional learning: A meta-analysis of school-based universal interventions. *Child Development, 82*, 405–432. doi:10.1111/j.1467-8624.2010.01564.

Dweck, C. S. (2006). *Mindset: The new psychology of success*. Ballantine Books.

Efklides, A. (2011). Interactions of metacognition with motivation and affect in self-regulated learning: The MASRL model. *Educational Psychologist, 46*(1), 6–25.

Fisher, D., & Frey, N. (2021). *Better learning through structured teaching: A framework for the gradual release of responsibility* (3rd ed.). ASCD.

Fisher, D., Frey, N., & Sax, C. (2004). *Inclusive elementary schools: Recipes for success* (2nd ed.). PEAK.

Flett, G. L., & Hewitt, P. L. (2014). A proposed framework for preventing perfectionism and promoting resilience and mental health among vulnerable children and adolescents. *Psychology in the Schools, 51*(9), 899–912.

Forber-Pratt, A. J., Merrin, G. J., Mueller, C. O., Price, L. R., & Kettrey, H. H. (2020). Initial factor exploration of disability identity. *Rehabilitation Psychology, 65*(1), 1–10. https://doi.org/10.1037/rep0000308

Friedman-Krauss, A. H., & Barnett, W. S. (2023). *The state(s) of early intervention and early childhood special education: Looking at equity*. National Institute for Early Childhood Education Research. https://nieer.org/sites/default/files/2023-10/se_fullreport.pdf

Fuchs, L. S., & Fuchs, D. (2006). Introduction to response to intervention: What, why, and how valid is it? *Reading Research Quarterly, 41*(1), 93–99. https://doi.org/10.1598/RRQ.41.1.4

Good, T. L. (1987). Two decades of research on teacher expectations: Findings and future directions. *Journal of Teacher Education, 38*(4), 32–47.

Haring, N. G., Lovitt, T. C, Eaton, M. D., & Hansen, C. L. (1978). *The fourth R: Research in the classroom*. Merrill.

Hattie, J. (2021, September 22). *An ode to expertise: What have we learnt from COVID and how can we apply our new learning* [Conference session]. Victoria Education State Principals Conference, Australia.

Hattie, J. (2023). *Visible learning: The sequel: A synthesis of over 2100 meta-analyses relating to achievement*. Routledge.

Hattie, J., Fisher, D., Frey, N., & Almarode, J. (2024). *The illustrated guide to visible learning: An introduction to what works best in schools*. Corwin.

Hattie, J., & Smith, R. (Eds.). (2020). *10 mindframes for leaders: The visible learning approach to school success*. Corwin.

Hattie, J., & Timperley, H. (2007). The power of feedback. *Review of Educational Research, 77*(1), 81–112.

Hattie, J., & Zierer, K. (2025). *10 mindframes for visible learning: Teaching for success* (2nd ed.). Routledge.

Heggerty, M. (2017). *Phonemic awareness: The skills they need to help them succeed!* Literacy Resources.

Hempenstall, K. (2020). Teaching reading through direct instruction: A role for educational psychologists? *The Educational and Developmental Psychologist, 37*(2), 133–139.

Howard, R. W. (2008). Linking extreme precocity and adult eminence: A study of eight prodigies at international chess. *High Ability Studies, 19*(2), 117–130.

Jones, S. M., & Bouffard, S. M. (2012). Social and emotional learning in schools: From programs to strategies and commentaries. *Social Policy Report, 26*(4), 1–33.

Joshi, G. S., & Bouck, E. C. (2017). Examining postsecondary education predictors and participation for students with learning disabilities. *Journal of Learning Disabilities, 50*(1), 3–13. https://doi.org/10.1177/0022219415572894

Jung, L. A. (2024). *Assessing students, not standards: Begin with what matters most.* Corwin.

Katsiyannis, A., Zhang, D., Ettekal, I., Chang, W., Li, P., Bigger, B., & Hullett, M. (2023). Minority representation in special education: 5-year trends from 2016–2020. *Advances in Neurodevelopmental Disorders, 9*, 23–36. https://doi.org/10.1007/s41252-023-00387-6

King-Sears, M. E., Stefanidis, A., Evmenova, A. S., Rao, K., Mergen, R. L., Owen, L. S., & Strimel, M. M. (2023). Achievement of learners receiving UDL instruction: A meta-analysis. *Teaching and Teacher Education, 122*, 103956.

Koedinger, K. R., Carvalho, P. F., Liu, R., & McLaughlin, E. A. (2023). An astonishing regularity in student learning rate. *Proceedings of the National Academy of Sciences, 120*(13), e2221311120.

Law, N., Hollins-Alexander, S., Hattie, J., March, A., Almarode, J., Fisher, D., Frey, N., Coote, L., & Tiatto, V. (2024). School climate and culture mind frames—Belonging, identities, and equity: A Delphi study. *International Journal of Educational Research, 125*, 102340.

Law, N., Hollins-Alexander, S., Smith, D., & Hattie, J. (2024). *Mindframes for belonging, identities, and equity: Fortifying cultural bridges*. Corwin.

Marsh, H. W., Chessor, D., Craven, R., & Roche, L. (1995). The effects of gifted and talented programs on academic self-concept: The big fish strikes again. *American Educational Research Journal, 32*(2), 285–319.

McIntosh, K., & Goodman, S. (2016). *Integrated multi-tiered systems of support: Blending RTI and PBIS.* Guilford Press.

Modica, M. (2015). *Race among friends: Exploring race at a suburban school.* Rutgers University Press.

Morgan, P. L., Woods, A. D., Wang, Y., Farkas, G., Hillemeier, M. M., & Mitchell, C. (2022). Which students with disabilities are placed primarily outside of U.S. elementary school general education classrooms? *Journal of Learning Disabilities, 56*(3), 180–192. https://doi.org/10.1177/00222194221094019

Ngo, F. J., & Velasquez, D. (2023). Inside the math trap: Chronic math tracking from high school to community college. *Urban Education, 58*(8), 1629–1657.

Nicol, D. J., & Macfarlane-Dick, D. (2006). Formative assessment and self-regulated learning: A model and seven principles of good feedback practice. *Studies in Higher Education, 31*(2), 199–218. https://doi.org/10.1080/03075070600572090

Nuthall, G. (2007). *The hidden lives of learners.* NZCER Press.

Oakes, J. (2005). *Keeping track: How schools structure inequality.* Yale University Press.

Oakes, J., Ormseth, T., Bell, R., & Camp, P. (1990). *Multiplying inequalities: The effects of race, social class, and tracking on opportunities to learn mathematics and science.* RAND.

Oakes, J., & Wells, S. A. (1996). Doing the right thing: The struggle to "detrack" secondary schools. *California English, 2*(1), 10.

Oregon Response to Instruction and Intervention. (2024). *MTSS-R component module series.* Oregon Department of Education. https://sites.google.com/nwresd.k12.or.us/mtss-rcomponentmoduleseries/

Peak Performance Center. (2024). *Mindsets.* https://thepeakperformancecenter.com/development-series/mental-conditioning/mindsets

Pianta, R. C. (1999). *Enhancing relationships between children and teachers.* American Psychological Association. https://doi.org/10.1037/10314-000

Popham, W. J. (2006). All about accountability/phony formative assessments: Buyer beware. *Educational Leadership, 64*(3), 86–87.

Pozas, M., & Schneider, C. (2019). Shedding light on the convoluted terrain of differentiated instruction (DI): Proposal of a DI taxonomy for the heterogeneous classroom. *Open Education Studies, 1*(1), 73–90.

Roebers, C. M. (2017). Executive function and metacognition: Towards a unifying framework of cognitive self-regulation. *Developmental Review, 45,* 31–51.

Rose, T. (2016). *The end of average: How we succeed in a world that values sameness.* HarperCollins.

Rubie-Davies, C. (2015). The teacher expectation project. *Character and Context.* https://spsp.org/news-center/character-context-blog/teacher-expectation-project

Rubie-Davies, C. M., & Hattie, J. A. (2025). The powerful impact of teacher expectations: A narrative review. *Journal of the Royal Society of New Zealand, 55*(2), 343–371.

Scarparolo, G., & MacKinnon, S. (2022). Student voice as part of differentiated instruction: Students' perspectives. *Educational Review, 76*(3), 1–18.

Schwab, S., & Woltran, F. (2023). Obstacles to Differentiated Instruction (DI) around the world. In V. Letzel-Alt & M. Pozas (Eds.), *Differentiated instruction around the world: A global inclusive insight* (p. 103). Waxmann Verlag.

Scriven, M. (1967). The methodology of evaluation. In R. W. Tyler, R. M. Gagne, & M. Scriven (Eds.), *Perspectives of curriculum evaluation* (pp. 39–83). Rand McNally.

Shanker, A. (1993). Alternative uses of ability grouping in secondary schools: Can we bring high-quality instruction to low-ability classes? *American Journal of Education, 102*(1), 1–22.

Shute, V. J. (2008). Focus on formative feedback. *Review of Educational Research, 78*(1), 153–189.

Steenbergen-Hu, S., Makel, M. C., & Olszewski-Kubilius, P. (2016). What one hundred years of research says about the effects of ability grouping and acceleration on K–12 students' academic achievement: Findings of two second-order meta-analyses. *Review of Educational Research, 86*(4), 849–899.

Subotnik, R. F. (2009). Developmental transitions in giftedness and talent: Adolescence into adulthood. In F. D. Horowitz, R. F. Subotnik, & D. J. Matthews (Eds.), *The development of giftedness and talent across the life span* (pp. 155–170). American Psychological Association. https://doi.org/10.1037/11867-009

Szumski, G., Smogorzewska, J., & Karwowski, M. (2017). Academic achievement of students without special educational needs in inclusive classrooms: A meta-analysis. *Educational Research Review, 21,* 33–54.

Tanner, K. D. (2012). Approaches to biology teaching and learning: Promoting student metacognition. *Life Sciences Education, 11,* 113–120.

Thrupp, M., Lauder, H., & Robinson, T. (2002). School composition and peer effects. *International Journal of Educational Research, 37*(5), 483–504.

Tomlinson, C. A. (2017). *How to differentiate instruction in academically diverse classrooms.* ASCD.

Tomlinson, C. A., & Imbeau, M. B. (2023). *Leading and managing a differentiated classroom* (2nd ed.). ASCD.

Wiliam, D. (2011). *Embedded formative assessment.* Solution Tree.

Winner, E. (2000). The origins and ends of giftedness. *American Psychologist, 55*(1), 159.

Yeager, D. S., Purdie-Vaughns, V., Garcia, J., Apfel, N., Brzustoski, P., Master, A., Hessert, W. T., Williams, M. E., & Cohen, G. L. (2014). Breaking the cycle of mistrust: Wise interventions to provide critical feedback across the racial divide. *Journal of Experimental Psychology: General, 143*(2), 804–824.

Zachary, L. J., & Fain, L. Z. (2022). *The mentor's guide: Facilitating effective learning relationships*. John Wiley & Sons.

Zhang, D., Katsiyannis, A., & Herbst, M. (2004). Disciplinary exclusions in special education: A 4-year analysis. *Behavioral Disorders, 29*(4), 337–347. https://doi.org/10.1177/019874290402900402

Zimmerman, B. J. (1989). A social cognitive view of self-regulated academic learning. *Journal of Educational Psychology, 81*(3), 329–339. https://doi.org/10.1037/0022-0663.81.3.329

Zingoni, M., & Corey, C. M. (2016). How mindset matters. *Journal of Personnel Psychology, 16*(1), 36–45. https://doi.org/10.1027/1866-5888/a000171

Index

CORWIN

To help every educator help every student

We believe that every single student deserves a great education

We believe that knowing our impact is both a privilege and a responsibility

We believe that a fair, stable, and thriving society is built on education

Zeitfracht Medien GmbH
Ferdinand-Jühlke-Straße 7
99095 Erfurt, Deutschland
produktsicherheit@kolibri360.de